MW00781459

Why this book is a must-read for people who want a bigger life ...

The people you know have the power to change your life and you have the power to change theirs. But what if meeting people isn't your strong suit? Or you've become complacent about making new connections? Or you simply do not know how you can live the powerful, fulfilled life you envision for yourself?

This life-changing book will underscore how powerfully connection supports your happiness, health and well-being, while also sharing practical ways you can find and make connections on a daily basis, almost anywhere.

In this zippy read, Jen Nash explains how the opportunity to connect is everywhere and how we can get more than we ever dreamed of out of life if we just make the effort to lean in and say hello.

Using amazing true-life stories and scientific research on how we listen, talk, and crave connection, this book demonstrates that making time to connect is the most productive thing we can do to thrive at home or at work.

Whether you want to go to more parties, get a better job, make more money, or get laid more—reading this book will give you practical strategies for doing it all. A happier, more successful, and more fulfilling life is within your reach. *The Big Power of Tiny Connections* will show you the way.

The Big Power of TINY CONNECTIONS

How Small Interactions Spark
Awesome Outcomes

by

Jen Nash

The Big Power of Tiny Connections -
How Small Interactions Spark Awesome Outcomes

Some of the names and identifying features of people in this book have been changed to protect their privacy.

Cover Design: Samantha Russo / srussodesign.com
Author Photograph: Joshua Xolox

Published by:

Big Shift Press
612 Bank Street, Suite 9
Ottawa, Ontario
CANADA K1S 1N6

ISBN eBook: 978-1-7779596-6-1/978-1-7779596-3-0
ISBN Paperback: 978-1-7779596-5-4/978-1-7779596-0-9
ISBN Hardcover: 978-1-7779596-2-3
ISBN Audiobook: 978-1-7779596-1-6

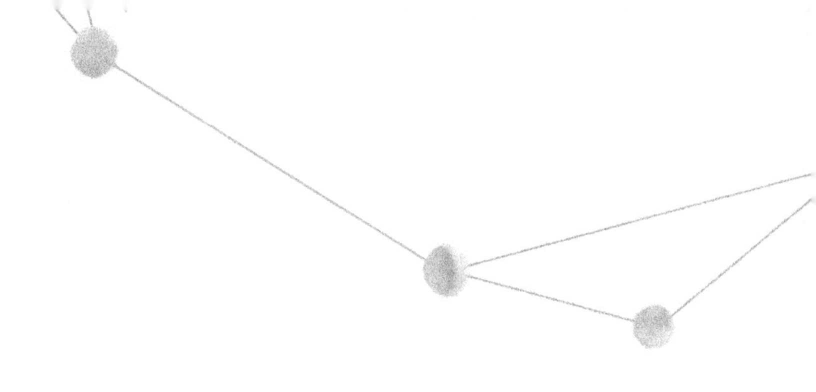

For Mom
who always knew I had a book in me
and for Sylvia
who lovingly hounded me long after Mom could not.

Contents

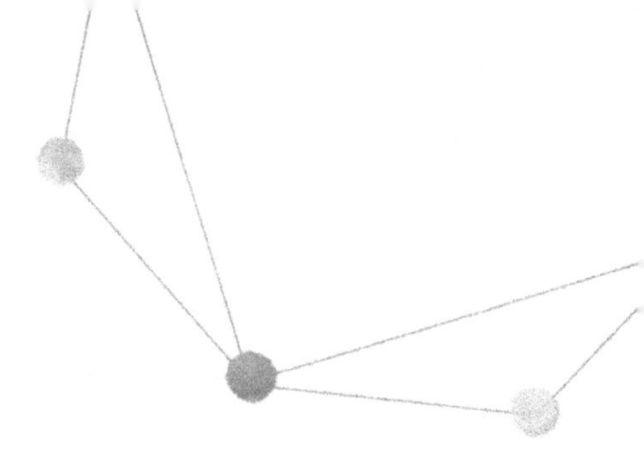

Prologue

My mother talked to strangers a lot. And while I didn't love it as a kid, I got used to it. I accepted the fact that she would strike up a conversation with pretty much anyone, anywhere. Mom would chat with the person next to us on the sidewalk while we were all waiting for the crosswalk light to change. She'd swap stories or recipe tips with the person in front of her in line at the butcher. She'd express interest in the server's childhood in Mumbai, India, or in a passerby's hand-quilted jacket from Little Rock, Arkansas, or in the intricate cane a gentleman in the art gallery was using. She'd share her historical, informational, medical, nutritional, or even spiritual advice with almost anyone, anywhere at any time.

Maybe this doesn't sound that odd, but she'd do it even if she didn't speak their language.

A Vassar graduate who focused her studies on languages, my mother spoke English, French, Spanish and German, picked up a smattering of Asian languages when we lived in Malaysia, Hong Kong, and Japan. If you didn't know her, watching her talk to random strangers would make you think she was the bravest, least inhibited person you had ever met. In truth, Mom was rather shy, but she buried that shyness under a mantle of bluster and personality.

As an adult, I would often be embarrassed when she would attempt to endear herself to the Asian shopkeepers in my New York City neighborhood. She'd walk into my local bodega and speak to the owners in Cantonese, since they looked Asian, and we'd spent many years living in Hong Kong. It might have worked, however most of the local shopkeepers in my area are Korean—not Chinese. These patient, kind-hearted shopkeepers didn't seem fazed by this elderly woman nattering to them in bits and pieces of some foreign language, as to them she was just another eccentric tourist, but I was mortified.

No matter my protests, Mom would carry on. She was certain she'd eventually not only get it right—but also make someone's day. And sure enough, once in a while she did. The look of surprise and astonishment on their faces would then be priceless. One minute here is the dotty older woman speaking nonsense and the next she's thanking them properly in their mother tongue. I asked my mom what the point of all the back and forth was, after all she could just politely thank them in English. She would just shake her head and point out the fact that by struggling, then making that unexpected connection across languages, she was sprinkling joy everywhere she went. Having seen the smiles some of them beamed at her as she walked away, I think she was onto something! Looking back, I don't know why I felt so impatient when Mom had these exchanges, because it was precisely these small moments that would lead me to understand how powerfully connective, motivating and supporting our interactions with the world can be— it was these moments that lead me to spend my time talking and coaching about the power of connection all over the world.

Over the years, the way my mother engaged with anyone and everyone, rubbed off on me. I started collecting thank yous in foreign languages: Arigato, Obrigado, Mootsomesk, Kitness—and those became my gateway drug to fast and easy connection. I have an uncanny ability to figure out where people are from, just by paying close attention to their accents. Many people think South Africans are Australian, or Brazilians are Argentinian—and they often don't know that people in Jordan speak Arabic. As I developed this skill, I realized that when I whip out the old "Chokran" (thank you) and "Masalema" (goodbye) in Arabic when I'm walking out of my local deli, the Jordanian deli owner Wadha always breaks into a killer smile. It never fails to put surprise and delight on his face!

Everything we have in our lives largely depends on the people we know and the people they know. So, the larger and more diverse your network is—the more unique, empowered, and amazing life you can lead. (By a diverse network I mean demographic diversity, paradigm diversity as well as skill and experience diversity.) Mom connected to make people's day. And while I enjoyed the flashes of connection that accompany my thank-you flexing, I realized there was so much more opportunity within those tiny sparks.

What's the Point?

Connection is extremely powerful. Transformative even. More than anything it's a tool we can use—or a muscle we can flex—to create the lives we want to live.

PART ONE

HOPING FOR CONNECTION

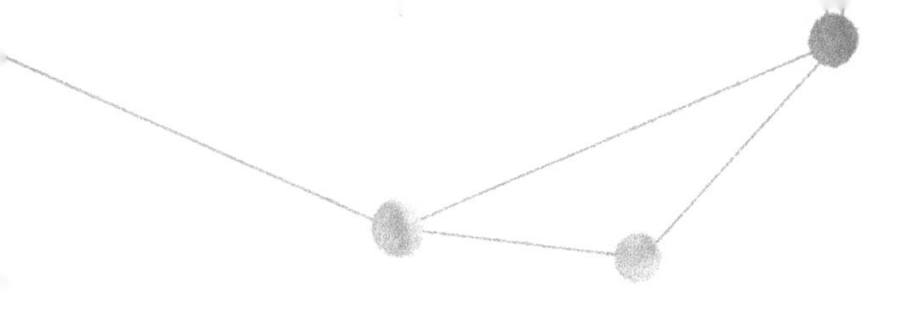

1

Tiny Connections ... Made to Be, Not Meant to Be

Liza, a particularly attractive friend of mine, was in a yoga studio waiting for the class to start. After fifteen minutes, it seemed the teacher was a no-show, so all the students started mulling about and chatting to each other. A young man in his mid to late twenties who had been sitting next to Liza, struck up a conversation with her for a few minutes and then casually asked if she had a Tinder handle. Since they were face to face, chatting away, Liza was curious why he wanted her online dating handle and asked him as much directly. He responded, "Well, I'd like to ask you out."

Let's think about this for a moment. Here we have a handsome 'yogi boi' standing next to Liza, and yet, he's become so reliant on apps to manage his social life he doesn't know how to ask a pretty girl out on a date without the intermediary assistance of technology. Liza was bemused and saddened, so she switched the topic of conversation and avoided giving him her number.

Nonetheless, the exchange shocked her enough that when she got home, she posted about the experience on Facebook—which is how I heard about it.

I remember being amazed and sad reading this story. How had dating evolved to such a place? As I thought more about it, I realized that a twenty-something-year-old has always lived in a world where there are dating intermediaries (websites, apps, etc.). He had never seen a personal ad in a newspaper or had to call someone (not text) to ask them out. It probably never even occurred to Yogi Boi to just ask Liza out on the spot. So, it got me wondering, how is a society that's hell bent on retreating into technology going to support creative human connections—the one thing we must have to live amazing, productive, lucrative, healthy, fulfilled lives? From where I'm standing, it seems like we're not only losing the ability to connect in person (sorry, Yogi Boi!) but we're losing the interest to connect at all, and that's really scary.

I Don't Just Talk the Talk: I Live and Breathe Connections

As a human connectivity expert, I travel the world, shifting people's perspective around the critical importance of human connections within their personal and professional lives. Through corporate and one-on-one executive coaching sessions, I focus on connection as the power base for excellence in leadership, inclusion and retention in a corporate world that's struggling with mass splintering.

Whether we're working onsite or remotely, the office culture of the past is just that … in the past. Now more than ever we must rethink how we connect with friends, family and coworkers as our days are jammed with video meetings and calls. I believe that you can't reap the social and financial benefits of connecting with others without the right kind of awareness, insights, and solid diligent effort. I know because I don't just talk about the power of connections, I live it.

I've been a creative director and marketing strategist for some of the most well-regarded companies in the world, which means I was paid very well to develop marketing campaigns that built relationships between people and brands. It also means I got very good at understanding human nature, because when you want people to take certain actions you must understand their motivations and make it very easy for them to take the steps you're hoping they'll take. While I was in this role, I was also simultaneously building a multi-million-dollar real estate portfolio. I knew nothing about real estate when I started in my early thirties, but I was extremely driven and focused on owning passive income properties—so I forced myself to meet a lot of people and asked a lot of questions so I could build a network of other real estate experts around me.

Over the years, I've transformed my career, grown my income well past six figures, befriended influential people and gained access to things I would never have seen or known about otherwise—all because I took concrete steps to connect with a wide range of people around me. I live the principles I'm espousing in this book, and as story after story will show you, nothing beats having awesome, life-changing experiences thanks to the connections you've made.

LET ME TELL YOU A STORY:

For my birthday, I historically have loved to go for high tea at a fancy hotel with someone who enjoys that sort of thing. I'm a fan of the petit fours, the tiny sandwiches, the scones, clotted cream and, of course, the excellent champagne. About a decade ago, my mother and I were having high tea at the Pierre Hotel, a classic New York landmark hotel, where I was planning to kick off my birthday week of silliness. We were sitting there enjoying the last sandwiches with our tea, when an older gentleman sitting nearby interrupted our conversation as he'd overhead us talking about living in Japan.

After asking us some questions about our experiences abroad, he politely begged our forgiveness for interrupting and went back to his drink. My mom and I however didn't want to let him off the hook so easily. He seemed smart, interesting, and fun! So instead of staying in our own lanes and minding our business, we invited him to join us.

It turned out he was not only the former mayor of a nearby large city but also the former governor of that state as well. He was very high energy and fun, and after twenty minutes or so, he invited us to join him for lunch two hours away at his home that was in a different state. Normally I don't drive two hours for lunch, but we were planning to head in that direction, as I lived part-time in New York and part-time in his state as well … so we accepted his invitation and met him the next day.

Over the following years, we've developed a friendship that has enabled me to meet and spend time at dinner with celebrities such as like Norah Jones, Tony Bennett and his gorgeous wife Susan Crow, as well other notables like the NBA commissioner Adam Silver and financial journalist Maria Bartiromo. I even got to meet Presidential Candidate Mike Bloomberg. It's amazing that one minute you're having tea and chatting and then less than a year later you're hanging out with celebs you normally only read about.

Connections Don't Just Happen

What do I mean by that? Well, for starters you can't just show up at some random bar and expect to be included with all the fun, attractive people. You can't sit back and wait for people to come to you. You must actively look for opportunities to connect and that's what I'm here to show you in this book. Step-by-step, I'm going to make it clear how you can create positive connections and outcomes in your life. I will help you see opportunities to connect where you currently see none. I'll inspire you to pay more attention to the world around you. To recognize the opportunities that cross your path every day, and to take action to turn those opportunities into amazing outcomes.

Making Tiny Connections Will

Get you a better job

How you interact at work can get you considered for promotions, unique opportunities, or juicy roles you wouldn't have thought possible.

Get you laid

People are more likely to be receptive to advances of any kind from people their peers have vetted. When you're introduced to someone through friends, you're instantly not a stranger and you've got instant street cred because of that lineage. That can make the leap from stranger to partner a much shorter affair. Pardon the pun!

Make you a person worth knowing

When you meet people, one of the first rules of being a good connection is asking yourself, "How can I help them?" "How can I make a positive change in their life?" It may be as small as giving them a tip about a good place to find parking, helping them get a babysitter for Saturday or sitting down over lunch to show them how to use Excel. When you make the world a better place, you'll find connecting gets a lot easier, and you'll likely feel great doing it.

Make you more money

While some of us are working hard to keep food on the table, it's possible some of the people you know (or the people they know) have access to deals, investment opportunities, IPOs, start-ups, you name it—and through them so do you. If you don't know any of those kinds of people, it's a great time to look at expanding your network.

Make your life more exciting

You weren't planning on ending up at the hottest party in Miami, but you got talking to someone at the bar, and one thing led to another—and there you are! You weren't planning to attend the Aspen Food & Wine Show, but you were open to working out a payment plan with a client, and they suggested taking you as their guest. With the right attitude toward making connections—you're more likely to get the corner office, marry an enviable partner, and have a social life that resembles the best alcohol commercials you've ever seen.

Turn you into a super-connector

When you introduce people for work or pleasure, and you facilitate new opportunities, friendships, or romances, you are supporting real growth and possibilities for those around you. This energy is addictive because it always comes back to support you and your goals.

Connection is Everything

Since 2018, I've been teaching and coaching connection, networking, leadership, and the powerful ways other people can change our lives. It may sound like an outlandish claim but our connection to people and the world around us is everything. Feeling a sense of connection is critical not only for your physical and mental wellbeing, but it's absolutely essential to live your best life. Think about a time a good friend cancelled plans with you last minute. How did you feel? Probably pretty bummed. Or think about how time spent alone in your apartment (perhaps during a pandemic quarantine) feels versus time spent at an intimate party with some of your closest friends. It's a wildly different experience, right?

Brené Brown is a research professor at the University of Houston who specializes in social connection. She is also an amazingly wise, funny, and successful best-selling author whose TED talks have been watched tens of millions of times. Brené shared[1]:

> *"A deep sense of love and belonging is an irresistible need of all people. We are biologically, cognitively, physically, and spiritually wired to love, to be loved, and to belong. When those needs are not met, we don't function as we were meant to. We break. We fall apart. We numb. We ache. We hurt others. We get sick."*

In a nutshell? Humans are profoundly social creatures. While it can seem like we all want power, money, beauty, fame, an Hermès necklace or a Tesla—at the root of most of these desires is our deep-seated yearning to be accepted, to belong, to be loved, and of course to connect deeply with others around us.

This need for connection starts when we're babies and lasts our whole lives. Babies who are not cuddled or hugged enough may stop growing at normal rates, and if the situation goes on long enough, they can even die. You don't have to look any further than the orphaned kids of Romania[2] that grew up unloved and uncuddled in orphanages between 1965 and 1989 to see the true nightmare our lives become when we are left alone, disconnected, and unloved from birth. Touch, connection, and real care are non-negotiable for the development of healthy humans.

A lack of connection kills

In the United States, loneliness rates have more than doubled in the last forty years, and 61 percent of American adults now report that they feel lonely.[3] In Japan, the number of seniors living alone increased more than six-fold from 1980 to 2015, and in 2018, over one million adults met the official government definition of hikikomori,[4] or a complete social recluse who never leaves their home. I don't know about you, but just reading that made me a little sad.

While a lack of connection, or social isolation, is not yet classified as a health condition by the medical community, a growing stack of research shows its astounding impact on our wellbeing. In fact, more and more studies[5] show that loneliness is the invisible root cause behind many health conditions, including addiction, depression, and heart disease—causing a 32 percent increased risk of stroke and doubling a person's likelihood of developing Alzheimer's.

One study found that social isolation leads to a higher risk of death, and it has an impact on our health that's similar to that of obesity, smoking fifteen cigarettes a day, excessive alcohol consumption, and a lack of physical activity.[6] Another report concluded that a lack of feeling connected can even make people more vulnerable to viruses like the common cold, the flu, or even COVID-19[7] because the resulting loneliness causes changes in gene expression in our white blood cells which result in reduced immune defenses.[8]

I think you'll agree that when you take all of this data into consideration—loneliness—or feeling a lack of connection, is a critical health issue. Our ability to connect, and create strong support systems, is linked to our health, our happiness, our success, our longevity, even to our thinner waistlines.[9] Here are more reasons why it's so important that we all form great connections.[10]

Strive for a healthy weight

Social support inversely correlates to your body mass index (BMI)—which is weight divided by height. That means that on average, the bigger your social network—the lower your BMI and weight will be. In a 2014 Journal of School Health study of 13,428 adolescents, children who felt more socially connected in their school environments tended to have lower BMI. A study of older Koreans found that those who had larger social networks with whom they interacted regularly had overall healthier weights.[11]

Boost your immune system

This may sound far-fetched, but human connection can even strengthen your immune system. Several studies have shown that better social support predicts how robust the immune response will be. For example, those who had more close connections, were less likely to catch the common cold.[12] Social support and stronger connections have also been linked to the antibody response that people have after they've gotten their flu shots. Turns out, the more human connection and support they have in their lives—the more antibodies they develop, and the more immunity they enjoy.[13]

Enjoy better mental health

Most of us understand that great relationships are the foundation of a happy life. We don't need science to tell us that. However, scientists have studied the link between human connection and mental health extensively. A 2014 Finnish study found that those with tighter social networks reported less loneliness and more positive emotions in their daily lives.[14] A wealth of other research suggests that loneliness can interfere with mental functioning, sleep, and well-being, which in turn increases the risk of illness and death.[15]

Live longer

According to a 2010 deep dive assessment of over 300,000 people, good social relationships were just as important for longevity as the avoidance of excessive smoking or drinking![16] Nuts, right? Not really. Think about it. Anyone who's connected to a strong social support network is more likely to engage in healthy behaviors like exercise, proper nutrition, and stress management. Strong human connection also fosters positive emotions, which in turn positively impact the body.[17]

We should prescribe social connection

Given the huge impact that loneliness and the lack of connection has on our mental and physical health—along with its hidden role in the development of so many chronic conditions—it seems logical that we need to hold the importance of connection in the same esteem as a healthy diet, regular exercise, not smoking, and obesity reduction.

One U.S. National Academies of Sciences, Engineering, and Medicine report suggested it was high time that health care professionals screened for loneliness. That it was time that governments and insurers fund research into loneliness' causes, effects, and cures; and that we needed to launch loneliness awareness campaigns targeted at people of all ages. There's also value in the idea that doctors and therapists need to 'prescribe' social connection in an effort to better link people to the resources and activities that can help them be less isolated.

Experts are predicting a skyrocketing loneliness crisis that will create a wave of mental illness, suicide, substance abuse, and violence borne of social isolation, especially for our loneliest populations: the young, the old, the poor, and immigrants. Knowing that, it would be helpful if we could destigmatize loneliness so that we are able to talk more openly about it when we feel disconnected—because this feeling is an expression of our innate human need to belong and connect. Loneliness is not a failure and should be something we feel comfortable talking to our family and friends about; doctors and therapists should bring it up too, and we probably could use some national campaigns to normalize and address the issue.

Connections Change Lives

Your personal human connections (the people you know from school, church, work, or your socials feeds) can not only keep you healthier and happier, they also have the power to get you a better job, a bigger paycheck, a better social network, or even just a better weekend. They may help you meet your future life partner, introduce you to your new best friend, or turn you on to the hobby that becomes your passion. Who you know dictates your life.

Love connections

According to a Facebook study, about 28 percent of college alumni ended up marrying their college boyfriend or girlfriend.[18] Princeton tour guides are often asked about their college cohorts' matrimonial prospects and they are known to offer up outlandish statistics. They'll happily exaggerate to prospective students by telling them that they're 75 percent likely to marry a Princetonian if they attend. However, with an insular campus social scene, annual reunions, and a network of alumni organizations in most major cities, realistic opportunities to find a special someone wearing Princeton orange are plentiful.[19]

Think college is a good place to connect to a mate? Wait until you get into the workplace. Almost 36 percent of employees have had a romantic relationship with a coworker and a third of work relationships result in marriage. Compared to relationships that start in bars or clubs, workplace romances are the most likely to end in a long-term commitment.

Work connections

LinkedIn research shows that a whopping 70 percent of people were hired at a company where they already had a connection in place.[20] That should be all the motivation you need to learn how to leverage your network to get referred by someone. At the most desirable companies such as Apple, Google, Facebook, Microsoft, or Instagram the number is even higher, with 95 percent landing jobs because of their connections. It makes sense when you think about it. Everyone wants to work with good people, so if you used to like working with someone at another company a few years ago it's easy for you to recommend them for a position at your current company. Plus, when people get a referral from someone they liked working with, they tend to take it more seriously. Your past experience with the candidate gives them a certain cachet if you will. Candidates whose resumes are submitted by someone the company knows have 20 times more chance of getting hired over someone who applied online. Anecdotally, it is logical that well-liked people get ahead. People who are known are hired faster than people who are not.

Lastly, networking at your company among other employees, makes you a better-known candidate when a promotion opportunity comes up. If recruiters can put a face to the name on the CV and already know your strengths from previous meetings, you're starting your application on a strong footing.[21]

As you dig deeper into understanding connection, you'll come to see how the humans around you have the power to make life so much more interesting, entertaining, and enriching, so it's critical you don't ignore or avoid your connection opportunities. In the next chapter, we'll delve into why so many of us hate talking to people we don't know well and why we'd rather get our nether regions waxed than hit that work function with our new team members. Why do we shy away from connecting with others and often opt for easy nights at home? I will map out ways to help you address those feelings of discomfort around meeting new people, and I'll provide simple strategies for overcoming that pesky imposter syndrome. (You know, when you feel like a fraud despite being smart, talented, and 100 percent capable.) I'll also address all the excuses that hold us back from really jumping into the mix of life.

What's the Point?

When you put effort into being curious about people, and work to get to know them, you'll uncover connections that can create unexpected, meaningful, and even magical bonds.

2

"I Don't Need More Friends" and Other Lies We Tell Ourselves

Most humans are not always up for talking to new people. We tell ourselves that "we don't need more friends or connections" in order to avoid having potentially awkward encounters with that little-known human species, humanis-strangis. However, as discussed in the last chapter, positive psychology makes a strong case that social relationships are the single most important predictor of people's well-being, and that people—with their powerful need to belong to social groups—cannot feel their best or be at their healthiest without having awesome, connective, and meaningful social relationships.[22]

When people have more conversations, they report increased feelings of happiness. Happy people tend to engage others more, so the cycle continues! It's not just when you're talking to friends or family, either—it turns out that chatting up a stranger is also good for your health.[23]

What's Really Holding Us Back?

Behavior change doesn't happen because a study says it should. We need to get to the root of our discomfort and tackle our fears one by one. Our concerns run much deeper than "I don't need more friends." Most of us have totally logical concerns when it comes to mingling with the unknown. The top fears most of us experience when even contemplating talking to humanis-strangis revolve around our fear that:

- we won't know how to start a conversation
- we won't enjoy talking to the stranger
- we won't like the stranger
- we'll run out of things to say
- they won't like us, and they'll run out of things to say

We humans worry a lot that the other person won't like us, instead of worrying whether we will like them. I hope the following intel[24] will allay some of your fears:

FEAR #1:
I Stress About All Aspects of Talking to Strangers

If you're worried about talking to strangers it's time to take a deep breath and push through it. That's easier said than done, but maybe it would help to know that most conversations with strangers go way better than either person expects. You'll feel more engaged than you expected, like them more than you expected, and neither of you will likely be bored or run out of things to say! People who don't stress about talking to strangers have less anxiety, less shyness, and tend to feel better about themselves in regards to their friends. So, I think we should all get on that train.

TAKE AWAY:
BE CURIOUS & COMPLIMENTARY

You want to ignore the knot you get in your chest when talking to strangers—but it's hard. The most hopeful way forward may be to accept that practice is required to overcome your discomfort. This is one of those instances in life, where you need to shut your eyes and jump in—with a curious and complimentary mindset. Get curious about their life, their stories, their past and present. Do so in an encouraging manner, and you'll both enjoy the chat.

FEAR #2:
I Can't Chitchat to Save My Life!

BELIEVE you're a great conversationalist and you'll become more likely to enjoy talking to strangers, and you'll BELIEVE the stranger will like you more. Arm yourself with the fundamental principles of good conversation (asking open-ended questions, listening attentively, and using good prompts like "What happened next?" or "Tell me more.") Have a basic knowledge of what's going on in the world so you'll have current topics to touch on when the conversation lulls. With these skills and a positive attitude, you will feel more confident and capable in all types of situations.

TAKE AWAY:
DON'T SECOND GUESS YOURSELF

Stay positive. If you're feeling uncomfortable, repeat over and over, "I'm a great conversationalist. People love talking to me." This type of positive reinforcement will drown out all the negativity that can run rampant in your mind when you get anxious. Don't give those little buggers the run of your brain. Take charge and keep it positive. Remember you've got hard data on your side.

FEAR #3:
Conversations with Strangers Suck

Nervous and think you need tips for better conversations? Nonsense!

TAKE AWAY:
TALKING TO STRANGERS CAN BE FUN

Once we dive in and get out of our own way—we kick ass. The fastest way forward? Staying positive and hopeful. I could give you all the tips in the world on how to start a conversation with a stranger, and how to keep engaging them in an enjoyable chat, and it won't make a difference to the outcome. Don't worry—I'll still give you the low down on easy conversations, just so you feel armed and ready to go—but according to several studies,[25] you'll end up having as good a chat with or without conversation tips. That's like knowing you're going to walk away from the roulette table a winner, regardless of whether you bet on red or black. I say, bet early and bet often!

What's Holding You Back?

So, if chatting with people is relatively painless, what's holding us back? Are we just lazy? Is it easier just to play Minecraft or Candy Crush on our phones? Certainly. So maybe what's holding us back the most is just making an effort, because, well, it's effort.

The voice in my head is pretty predictable when I'm supposed to be heading off to interact with anyone I don't know all that well.

> *Do I honestly need more friends?*
> *Do I really need to get to know my co-workers better?*
> *Why would I go out? I'm tired and I can't be bothered.*
> *I've got too much going on, I can't get my head in 'social' mode.*
> *I don't have time for anything besides work, family, and the gym!*

That little voice yammers on and on, talking me out of meeting new people all the time. It tempts me with a night on the couch, watching billionaire entrepreneurs stab each other in the back. Or puppy pictures on Instagram. However, nights spent communing with digital services aren't going to help me level up, infuse my world with meaning, or fill my life with purpose—and they certainly aren't going to offer up unexpected plot twists.

Knowing that the urge to bail on even the stuff you actually want to do is a powerful force to be reckoned with—how can you motivate yourself to walk out the door? What's the right mindset that will keep your enthusiastic momentum alive?

A Connective Mindset? Yes!

What kind of mindset do you need to shake your tail feather around strangers, or at least put on pants (with a real waistband) and engage with people? An open one. Open-mindedness typically means you have to be open to new ideas, different perspectives, and new experiences. You need to embrace one big fat YES!

Throughout this book, you'll hear true stories about people who said YES. For example, a woman befriends a stranger in a grocery store, and the two discover a connection that will blow your mind. Stay aware of the options and opportunities around you. Actively pursue connective moments—because amazing connections are everywhere, but they won't just fall into your lap without your massive, enthusiastic, and energetic YES! You also have to be curious, kind, and very present.

By now you're starting to see why you should adopt a SUPER YES mindset—it's fun and can lead to magical experiences. Curious as to when is a good time to seize your next opportunity to spark a new connection? I've got some helpful ground rules:

1. **Any time another adult offers you something you want.**

   Perhaps someone offers you a ride home late at night and you live far away. Maybe someone invites you out to meet their friends who are visiting from Ireland. Or maybe they offer you a tour of their newly designed office because you're an architecture buff. Whatever is offered, don't spend a single minute second-guessing what people offer. They are adults and know what they are doing so take them up on it if it sounds like it might be interesting. At the very least, see the offer for what it is at its core: an opportunity to spend time connecting with someone.

2. **When strangers are doing something that you'd like to do.**

   Who cares if it's the opposing softball team that's going for drinks at that cool new Tex-Mex place downtown? So what if you don't know anyone going? You've been meaning to check the place out—why not do it while making a few new friends? A simple "Hey I know I don't know any of you all that well … but mind if I tag along?" will likely get you a favorable response. Yes, it's uncomfortable, but not for long. Take a deep breath, and get yourself included!

3. **When people ask for help.**

   Maybe someone high-up at work is looking for extra support on a project over the weekend, or maybe someone from your condo association needs a quick favor—if your schedule permits it, volunteer. Never underestimate where these moments can lead, or which doors they can open.

I wish every opportunity announced itself with an embossed, letterset invitation—but life doesn't work that way. Opportunities come when you're talking to someone in the supermarket checkout line. When you're at the Department of Motor Vehicles. When you're lying by the pool at a fancy hotel in Maui. They even come when you're pushing your bike down a desolate road looking to get a flat tire fixed! Whatever form the opportunity takes—say YES!

LET ME TELL YOU A STORY:

Mitch was a young guy growing up in Sydney in the early nineties. While he loved his hometown, it felt very small to him in many ways and the cultural scene often felt repressed. He'd fantasized about moving to New York City where he knew he could more fully express himself as a well-rounded creative. While in his early twenties, he worked in PR and was fascinated by the mix of art, politics, and sexuality that he was reading about in magazines like PAPER and The Village Voice. Very much into the night-life scene, he eventually found himself dancing at Sydney's biggest party of the year—Mardi Gras. Thousands of handsome gents had poured into the city from around the world to dance for days. Next thing Mitch knew he was chatting to a New Yorker, to whom he wistfully confided, "I would love to live in New York City!" Moments later, Mitch had an open invitation to come crash in NYC. What did he do? He finished college in three months, saved up money, and moved to New York where he still lives twenty-five years later. He told a random stranger what he wanted, and in that moment the stars aligned, and his dreams came true.

One way to get in a SUPER YES mindset is to hang with others who enjoy connecting with new folks. Do you have a friend in sales who has no issues schmoozing a room getting to know everyone? Is one of your relatives the town matchmaker and hears everyone's business? People who like people have an energy that you can emulate. Jump in on the action. Watch them. Take mental notes. How do they get in and out of conversations gracefully? How do they make the person they're talking to feel heard, seen, and appreciated? Do as they do, with all the YES you can rally.

What's Your Motivation?

Putting yourself out there requires motivation on all fronts. You have to leave whatever comfort you're currently enjoying and seek out the company of those who have the potential to radically change your life. Yet—we're human so we can't help but be hesitant, lazy, and resistant to pushing ourselves.

How do I motivate myself to connect more? I have a couple of approaches. For instance, sometimes I bribe myself. Sometimes I negotiate with myself. Or sometimes, I give myself a series of hoops to jump through. I've come up with tactics and tricks that will motivate me off the couch, out of the office, and out into the wild world. Try this the next time you want to bail on going out:

- I'll go for an hour and a half, THEN I can go home and do whatever I want.
- I'll head home when I've gotten five new business cards.
- I'll bail when I've had three really enjoyable and connective chats with people I don't know.
- I'll leave after I've met someone who has taken a

vacation in Croatia, and who can give me some great tips for my next adventure. (This kind of information scavenger hunt can make for a fun way to network a room. You simply ask a lot of people a very direct question: Have you been to Croatia? If they say no, you just say thank you and move on! Trust me, it's a fantastic way to do-si-do around a gathering.)

- Reward yourself for going out with treats waiting for you at home. Maybe you can watch the next episode of your favorite show. Maybe you get cheesecake.
- If I'm feeling particularly unmotivated, I drag a friend out. I'll explain to them that I need to meet new people, and we'll scan the room together, identifying who we'll talk to. Mind you, your friend has to be game for this adventure, so warn them ahead of time of your plan.
- Is the call of the couch a strong one? It's time for a pep talk! Remind yourself of all the cool stuff that MAY happen if you go out. You may meet someone that will help you up the corporate ladder. Or you may meet someone who's an expert at that thing you've always wanted to try, or they'll know someone you've been trying to connect with.

These are just some ideas to get you thinking about what might work for you. What could you promise yourself as a reward for a connection well made? What trade off would you give yourself for spending an hour at that work function, when you really just wanted to blow the whole thing off? Sometimes it's just a matter of getting a little fancy so you feel good inside and out, then putting on your shoes and walking out of the house with a 'there's no turning back' attitude. Or if that sounds like too much effort—skip the dressing up and just go.

I'm a fan of the 'just do it' mentality. The well-regarded motivational speaker Mel Robbins has a five second concept. If you're not going to do something within five seconds, like get up when the alarm rings—then you're probably not going to do it. So, when someone suggests you hit a poetry slam, or a softball game—don't hesitate. Just go. Say YES. It's harder to weasel out of a commitment once it's made. It also helps to stop thinking about meeting other people as work. It's fun! It's not work. It might be life changing. So, get your head in gear, and figure out how best to motivate yourself.

A Look at What Holds Us Back

Here is a list of other ways we justify avoiding new interactions. Scan down this list and see which ones resonate with you, then skip ahead, and read how to approach your particular hesitation. Next time you're debating whether to go to something, you'll not only recognize the voice in your head that's holding you back, but you'll respond to it appropriately.

Classic List of Excuses:

1. Going out is a waste of time. No one wants to meet me, talk to me, or help me.
2. I already know all the real players in my industry/ company.
3. Everyone wants to meet me, and I want to meet no one.
4. I don't have time, I'm just too busy.
5. I'm tired, lazy, or I'd rather just stay home.
6. I can't be bothered to put myself out there.
7. I'm scared they won't like me.
8. I don't like shallow chitchat; it feels like I'm wasting my time.

The best way to defuse excuses and fears is to address them head on. Decide which ones resonate with you, and take a look at how you can adjust your behavior accordingly.

1. Going out is a waste of time. No one wants to meet me, talk to me, or help me.

This is probably the most common excuse I've heard. Can you relate to the idea that no one wants to meet you? That no one will find you interesting? That no one will want to help you achieve whatever goals you might have? Well, with that kind of attitude, I dare say you're probably right.

No one likes a sorry sap. Instead, buck up baby, wipe your tears, put on a bold, happy face, and get out there! You believing in you is the only thing that matters. You wanting to help yourself and others is the only thing that's going to move your needle. And you trusting that you're interesting and of value is the main contributing factor to actually being that. Don't believe me? Research shows that nearly 70 percent of people are plagued with feelings of self-doubt, often called imposter syndrome.[26] Imposter syndrome is a pattern where someone doubts their skills, talents, or accomplishments so they suffer from a constant internalized fear of being exposed as a 'fraud.'

Sheryl Sandberg, the COO of Meta Platforms Inc. (formerly known as Facebook) and the founder of LeanIn.org, has admitted that she often felt like an imposter. She wrote in her book *Lean In:* "Every time I took a test, I was sure that it had gone badly. And every time I didn't embarrass myself—or even excelled—I believed that I had fooled everyone yet again. One day soon, the jig would be up." She has often shared with the media that, despite having gotten into Harvard's honor society, Phi Beta Kappa, she didn't feel like she deserved to be there. In an interview about *Lean In*, Sandberg shared, "There are still days when I wake up feeling like a fraud, not sure I should be where I am."

While you might think that fame and success would reassure someone with huge talent and followers, sometimes self-doubt can still creep in. David Bowie is quoted as saying, "I had enormous self-image problems and very low self-esteem, which I hid behind obsessive writing and performing … I really felt so utterly inadequate. I thought the work was the only thing of value."

In her documentary, *Five Foot Two*, Lady Gaga says, "I still sometimes feel like a loser kid in high school, and I just have to pick myself up and tell myself that I'm a superstar every morning so that I can get through this day and be for my fans what they need for me to be."

While movie screen stunner Penelope Cruz shared, "I feel every time I'm making a movie, I feel like [it's] my first movie. Every time I have the same fear that I'm gonna be fired. And I'm not joking. Every movie, the first week, I always feel that they could fire me!"

Many people talk about 'faking it, until you make it' to overcome imposter syndrome. I'm a massive fan of this approach. Don't listen to that voice in your head. You've got a lot to offer, go out and offer it! You never know where your initiative will lead. But if you can't pep talk your way into a better state of mind, do the following:

Stop talking and take action. Rather than try to convince yourself you can do better, give it a shot. Even if you initially fail, action is motivating and encourages you to try again—which of course increases your odds of success and gets your thoughts headed in the right direction. As humans, we like to overthink things. By jumping in and doing the thing you are nervous about you're taking a stand and making tangible efforts.

Focus on your past successes. Take stock of what you've done well. Make a list of your achievements and when you hit a mental roadblock, review your past wins. Reminding ourselves that, "We've got this" goes a long way to keeping us moving forward.

Celebrate each win, big and small. If you're stuck in a pit of self-doubt, you can become consumed by it. It's easy to blow insecurities out of proportion. Try to notice when you have negative thoughts and realize they are just that—thoughts. Focus on the small wins, and the momentum built by those tiny changes can add up quickly. Make notes about what's working and where you're feeling good. Identify what you're doing to support the good, and do more of that. This will help you keep tabs on your wins. What we focus on will grow, and pretty soon you'll have more wins. So, if you realize on days you meditate, you have less anxiety and more patience for the people around you … meditate more often. If on days you have that third cup of coffee you're more irritable and less open minded … skip that last coffee.

2. I already know all the real players in my industry/ company.

I find that when people are this brazen, and confident, it's probably true. You probably do know all the players, and you're pretty bored with how things are currently. Maybe it's time to branch out. For instance, if you work in manufacturing, you could start to meet new people in the world of shipping and distribution, or in other facets that positively affect your work in manufacturing.

Being powerful and well connected has a certain appeal, but living in your head, and resting on your laurels will eventually get boring. Life shouldn't be stagnant! That means it is likely high time you start to meet new people in different areas of life that interest you. You can't rely on meeting people only at work, or only at the gym, or only at church. Look at your life holistically and see where you have an opportunity to dive deeper.

If you love music, you could start attending music festivals and mingling with other like-minded music lovers. Maybe you aspire to be an artist? Perhaps a weekend art class supplemented with museum tours could be the way forward to meet other people who share your passion and who will add dimensionality to your life. It's possible that making artistic friends improves your life at work in unexpected ways. Perhaps you're in a better mood, so you're kinder. Maybe you'll be more likely to support different creative avenues at work. You simply never know how the different people you'll meet will contribute, improve, or even expand your current world.

3. Everyone wants to meet me, and I want to meet no one.

When you've made it, however you define that, people will want to talk to you. They will line up after you've given a talk to shake your hand, ask you questions and connect with you. They will want to work with you and for you. They will also want you to help them achieve their dreams. Is it any wonder that you might not want to socialize? You feel as if the world is tugging on your sleeve, needing you to do them favors while you're wondering: What's in it for me?

I'll tell you what's in it for you. New friends. New adventures. New opportunities. New awareness. When you self-select out of engaging with others, you're missing the opportunity to expose yourself to new perspectives and the personal growth that goes along with that. That's not to say that it's easy to weed out the clingers from the genuine souls, but by keeping an open mind, you're staying in the game.

4. I don't have time. I'm just too busy.

Fair enough. Sometimes life really is just too busy and you're too overwhelmed. Maybe you work several jobs, have a lot of family commitments, friends, and sporting activities. Maybe meeting new people just isn't all that important. No biggie. There is a time and a place for everything.

That said, it's a good idea to ask yourself if you're feeling fulfilled by your career and how things are going on that front. I hope your friend group is meeting all your needs for love and connection. That your family is as present for you as you are for them. Because if the answer to any of these was not a resounding YES, it may in fact be time to branch out and expand your connections. You may also want to take a closer look at your relationships, to see if you're staying connected because you feel obligated, or because you've always been in each other's lives. Obligation and habit aren't good reasons to keep people in your life, especially when you need your energy for new and exciting connections.

You might want to start making time, once a week, to get out there. Go to events. Conferences. Or if going out into the real world isn't possible, for whatever reason, it's time to jump into Facebook, Reddit, Quora, or other online groups and start connecting with like-minded humans. Maybe you set aside time every day to read articles on topics that interest you, then connect with the authors. Connections don't need to be in person to be powerful and effective, they just need to have that wonderfully elusive gel that brings liked minded people together. Not sure how to connect? Telling them what you liked about their piece and asking for advice can start a dialogue going.

If you are working several jobs while juggling kids and family, it's possible you really don't have time. However, for many of us, the 'I don't have time excuse' often really means you're simply not that interested in doing whatever it is you are avoiding. We all make time for a million things that aren't life or death. Baking cookies with the neighbor's kids. Taking a bike ride with the family. Watching the news before work. Having a long talk on the phone with an old friend. We do all those things because we WANT TO, not because we have to. Thus, I find the 'I don't have time' excuse to be a cop-out. You have the time; you just really don't want to go out. Better to address that about yourself head on, and not make excuses.

5. I'm tired, lazy, or I'd rather just stay home.

This excuse is my personal downfall. I worked two jobs for almost two decades and that work sucked-up most of my days and part of my weekends. It's no wonder that I often struggled to feel enthusiastic to do anything after work, especially if it was work related. I don't want to make an effort to connect with random strangers, especially when I really don't have any guarantees I'll ever meet anyone interesting. Sound familiar? Of course, it does. We're all human.

However, if that was how I always lived my life, I wouldn't have landed my first internship at Kirshenbaum & Bond, one of the hottest ad agencies in New York City back in the '90s. While I was still in college and working two jobs to pay for my rent and all my art school expenses, I forced myself to go to events hosted by The One Club for Creativity, a creative club of copywriters and art directors that often hosted events to showcase the work of different ad agencies. It was at one of The One Club events, while standing in front of an overwhelming cheese plate that I met Peter, a tall, charming strategist with a killer British accent, who was looking for an intern to help him build a client database. I'll admit that I'd consciously planted myself beside all that cheese, because I figured the cheese would give me a good conversational ice breaker. Sure enough, when Peter came over to also inspect the spread, I think I said something brilliant and witty like, "It's a lot of cheese don't you think?" Or I might have asked, "I'm hoping there is some Gouda somewhere on this platter. What do you think? Anything look like Gouda to you?"

Either way—my ploy worked, and we quickly got talking. Once I learned he was looking for an intern, I immediately volunteered for the unpaid position; despite the fact I knew nothing about databases and that I had hoped to land a creative internship that would give me the opportunity to write ads and work with art directors. However, once I'd worked for Peter for several months, and started meeting the rest of the agency, I realized how easy it was to offer my services to the creative directors and try to see what small little tidbits they might want a junior writer to help out on. Sure enough, I ended up getting to write a little promotion piece for Solgar vitamins, which put me over the moon. Plus, over the course of the next year, I made friends in that ad agency who changed my life.

One such friend invited me years later to the coolest wedding in England, while another became my first freelance client and ended up paying one of my invoices with an all-expense paid trip to the Aspen Food and Wine event. Talk about interesting connections! And none of that would have happened had I stayed home instead of schlepping out to that One Club event. If you're leaning toward having a chill night in on your couch, think about the things you want to adjust in your life, or the things you aren't satisfied with, and go out with the intent to help find interesting solutions.

While you're at it, remember to stay open-minded. I didn't want to work in business development or strategy—but I took the internship anyway … and it paid off in spades.

6. I can't be bothered to put myself out there.

I don't know if this is just the lazy excuse. Or the fear excuse. But either way, it doesn't move you, your dreams, or your fun barometer forward. Maybe reach a little deeper inside of yourself to get a better sense of what's going on, because this type of response is usually superficial. You're going to laugh, but consider grabbing a pen and write about 'why you can't be bothered' for ten minutes. Journaling can uncover a lot of interesting thoughts and buried emotions.

Is it fear of rejection? That's understandable. Could it be fear of feeling lonely and left out while you stand there not talking to anyone? That's also understandable. But in the end, living in our little pre-existing, status-quo boxes is boring without the added joy, silliness, brilliance, creativity, intellect, and hilarity that others add.

7. I'm scared they won't like me.

Fear is paralyzing. Sometimes the notion that no one wants to talk to us is NOT all in our heads. Case in point: I used to be a financial reporter for a very well-respected financial publication, and I can assure you that when I went to conferences, NONE of the high-level investment bankers wanted to talk to me. For reasons of job security and industry reputation, these intensely private finance types couldn't even be seen talking to a reporter. I guess they were worried that if someone saw us chatting, they would get accused of spilling the beans about some ultra-secret $100 million-dollar building acquisition that wasn't public yet. At these conferences, I was literally a social pariah—someone to avoid at all costs. At this point in my life, I was twenty-six years old and I can assure you, knowing that at a conference of 2000 people no one wanted to be seen with you, talk to you, or even sit near you at a hotel bar was a major downer. I definitely spent a few moments puddled in self-pity, hiding out in my hotel room.

But unless you're a reporter surrounded by finance types, it's unlikely that no one will like you. So don't get too dramatic. Put on your most unusual shirt, skirt, shoes, or pocket square, and go mingle! (Never underestimate the value of giving people something easy to comment on: "Damn that's a funky pocket square you got there!" "Purple tights? I like it." "Where did you get that shirt? It's giving me rainbow flashbacks!") The worst thing that could happen is you end up having an excellent chat with whoever is pouring what's on tap! Waitstaff can often be illuminating, so that's really not a bad night out after all. Maybe you too will end up in Panama City.

Not into leaving the house? We'll touch on virtual mingle sessions throughout the book, but many of the same premises apply.

8. I don't like shallow chitchat; it feels like I'm wasting my time.

Here's my thought on lame, vapid chitchat. It is lame, and it is vapid, so don't do it. You're 50 percent in charge of how the conversation is going, so take ownership of your part of this charade. If you don't like talking about work, the weather, or whatever you are doing this weekend, ask better questions. You can pre-frame your question by telling whomever you are speaking to that you don't like idle chat—or you can dive right in:

- "Where's the coolest place you've ever been?"
- "I'm not a fan of superficial chatter: So, let me ask you: do you think God exists?"
- "Do you prefer red sauce or white? On your pasta I mean."
- "Is love at first sight a real thing?"
- "True or False: Our ears keep growing for our whole lives?"

- "What's your superpower?"
- "I hate idle chitchat, let's talk about something meaningful. When was the last time you took criticism to heart?"

I love the fact that if you toss a zinger like these at someone in a very status-quo kind of environment, you will typically get a laugh, a raised eyebrow and at the very least the energy of the moment will be elevated. I'm not at all interested to talk about the latest OS software updates or where my kids go or don't go to school ... I would much rather shake things up and talk about the secret to the perfect crepe or how to wake surf without losing your bikini top. Take the lead, and bat down the casual banter that keeps most of us bored stiff in new introduction situations. Think of fun questions that make you smile and get on with it. Who knows, maybe you'll end up in a passionate discussion about weird things that have happened while you were a guest in someone's home, or the best way to get out of a speeding ticket.

Strangers—Your One-Way Ticket to the Life You Want

Sure, there's endless reasons why you don't want to meet new people, but if you want to make more money, have more fun, and live a better life, you're quickly going to see the benefits of spending more time in your less-than-comfortable zone. In the following chapters, I'll show you how making connections can and will change your life in exactly the ways you're hoping.

What's the Point?

Amazing connections are everywhere, but they won't just fall in your lap without a massive, enthusiastic, and energetic SUPER YES. Adopt that mindset today, and you'll start to see connective opportunities everywhere.

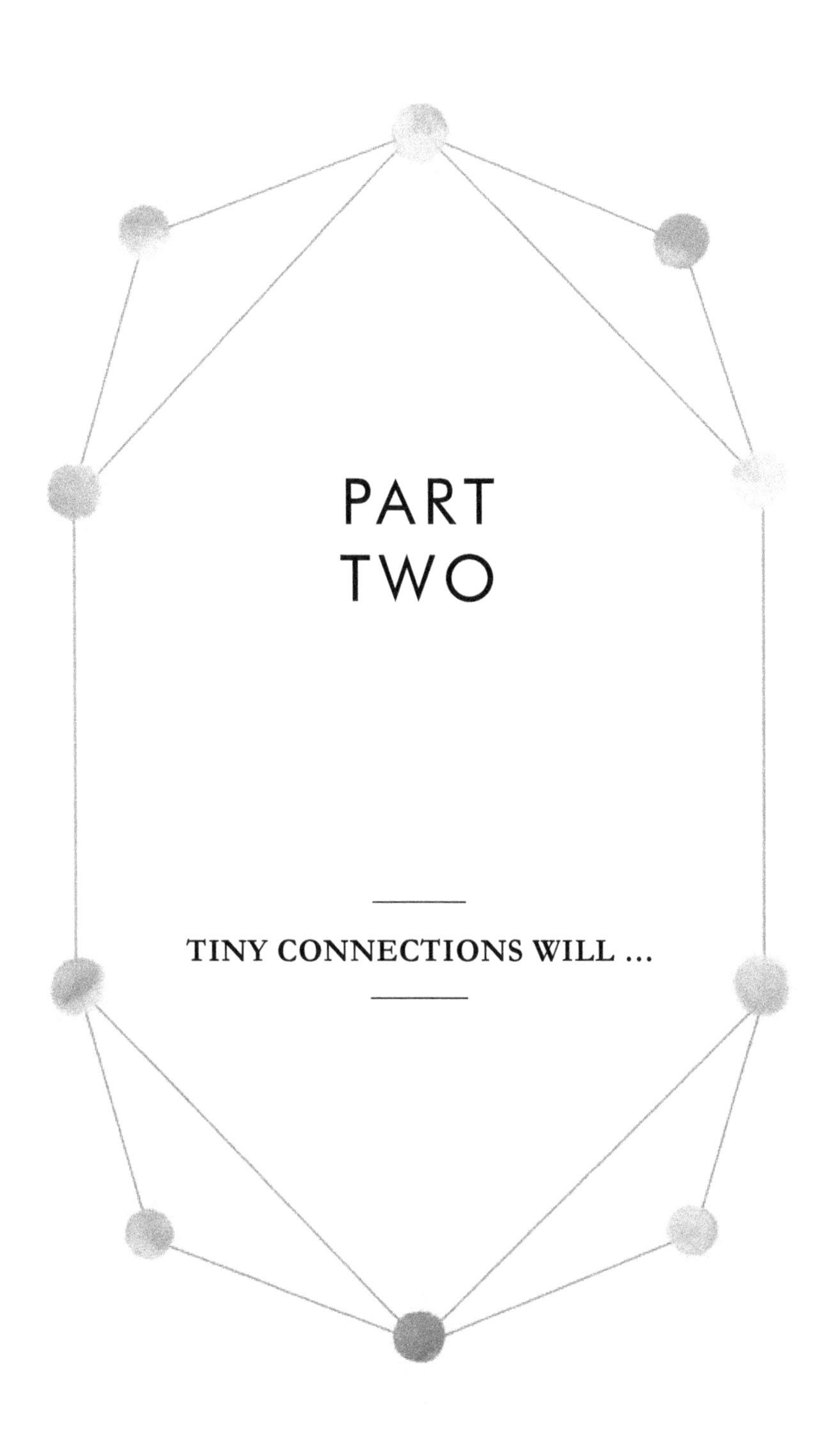

PART TWO

TINY CONNECTIONS WILL …

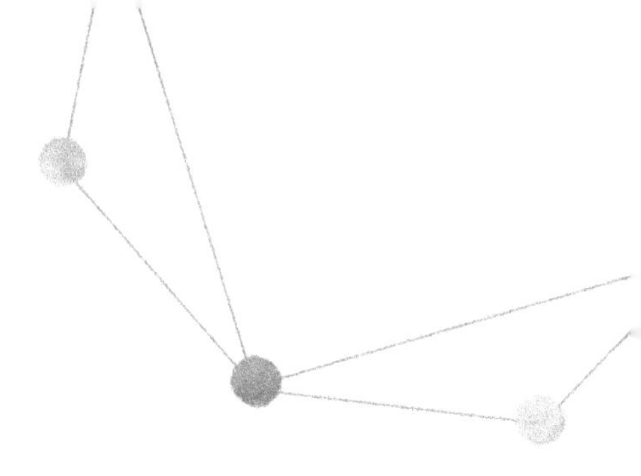

Tiny Connections Will ...

Life can be monotonous without the unexpected little variations that new connections, unexpected encounters, and random acts of kindness deliver. You can sit down next to someone at a dinner party, on a bus or plane, and an hour later, the two of you are sharing incredibly personal stories, recounting wild adventures, or exchanging health tips.

When you snuggle into the couch with a dear friend you've known forever, it's like a cozy sock. You have a well-established social dynamic. It's wonderful. Powerful. Loving. But it's typically not going to change your life, expand your horizons, or evolve your world perspectives—because you already know each other so well. You know what not to talk about, and what is safe ground. But with strangers? I'm not going to say the sky's the limit because we still have to be mindful of etiquette and current hot-button topics, but we may have more license than we realize, and that's exciting. Who knows where things will go? You could end up moving to a foreign country, changing jobs, or being an extra in a movie that's shooting down the street. Literally anything can happen.

What do I mean by anything can happen? Well, embracing the tiny connection mindset will shift your whole life, in almost any way you want. In the chapters to come, we'll delve into some of the awesome (and even potentially life-changing) outcomes you can create for yourself. For instance, if you've always wanted to be the life of the party—and get invited to more parties—we'll make that happen. Want to make more money? Or get a better job? Guess what, 80 percent of jobs and pay raises have to do with who you know and what they think of you. If you want to add a bit more romantic spice to your life, improving your connection capacity can make that a reality. If you'd just like to up your 'awesome human' game while on planet earth, I'll give you friend changing, behavior evolving, and life improving pointers. If you're ready to live a healthier, happier, more connected life—step right this way.

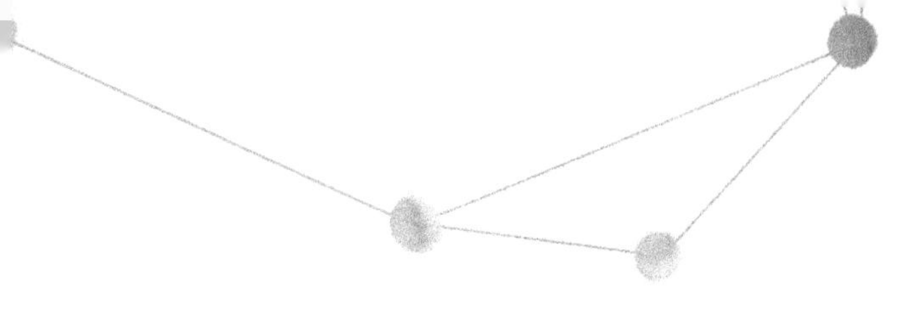

3

Tiny Connections Will ... Make You Interesting at Parties

Being an interesting and engaged party guest is a great goal. After all, no one wants energetic duds at their events, so if you care to up your tiny connection game, you'll be adding something valuable to any gathering in no time. How does one go about being an awesome invitee? No outrageous outfits, endless hostess gifts, or fire juggling skills are required (although they never hurt). There is really just one thing you need in order to have the best time, mingle with the most guests, make potentially life-changing connections, and get invited back again and again. You need to be interesting.

One of the grounding principles of connecting with others is having the fundamental self-confidence that you are a person worth knowing. Ask yourself: Am I worth knowing? Do I think I'm interesting?

Hopefully your answer is a resounding "YES!" But if you are hesitant, not to worry. There is another way forward that doesn't require you to ride camels across the Sahara under a full moon, jump out of a plane over Mont Blanc, France, or race Enduro cars around a dirt track in the backwoods of Pennsylvania, USA. (Although doing fun, unique things like these is always a great conversation starter!) No, the key to making everyone think you're interesting is well documented: be interested in them. Get curious about them, because when you do, they open up, get talking, and feel great. When they feel great—they like you. A lot.

We LOVE to Talk About Ourselves

On average, people spend 60 percent of conversations talking about themselves—and this figure jumps to 80 percent when communicating on social platforms like Instagram or Facebook. We live in a world full of ideas to uncover, dissect, and develop—so why do people spend most of their time talking about themselves? We do it because it feels good.

The Harvard University Social Cognitive and Affective Neuroscience Lab did a study[27] where they stuck people into magnetic resonance imaging (MRI) machines and got them talking about different subjects from both their own point of view and the point of view of others. Guess which subject lit up the areas of the brain that are generally associated with feeling good or rewarded, and that have been linked to the pleasurable feelings people enjoy from stimuli like good food, sex, or cocaine? If you guessed sharing their own point of view, you'd be right. They also deduced that knowing someone was listening is important to us and to our brains. It makes us feel good.

Armed with that knowledge, how do you get people talking about themselves with ease? In a nutshell, you have to get curious. But what does that really mean?

Let's Get Curious

A relationship coach I was talking to in New York recently suggested that one of the most amazing things you can do to support and transform any relationship is: GET CURIOUS. Instead of jumping to judgment about something being good or bad, ask questions around why something was that way. So, if you've just found out someone hasn't left the house in several days, you may be tempted to react by saying, "Oh no! That's terrible." But if you respond with, "Wow. Tell me about that. What's going on?" It's more likely that you'll understand the other person, without getting their guard up.

While that may sound a little new-agey, I love that idea because it engages that child-like part of ourselves that will never grow up and is always hoping for a sprinkling of magic in the world. It's our curiosity that drives us to discover, uncover, explore, create, ideate, imagine, and so much more.

How can you get curious in your day-to-day life? Well, you can start by asking someone questions. Put on your wide-eyed-four-year-old lenses, and ask them why they feel the way they do about something. Why they love or don't love something. How or why they are becoming a blogger, learning to make their own sourdough starter, or spending their time working on race cars … or anything else that comes to mind. While this can be a very kind, supportive, and loving behavior to try in existing relationships, it's an extremely bold, unexpected, and fun move to pull with strangers. Nothing says 'I am actively taking an interest in you' like someone being curious about you. When people take an interest in you—it feels great! When they ask about your work, your family, or about your personal interests, beyond lighting up your brain's pleasure reward centers, it makes you feel seen, heard, and possibly even valued. Plus, everyone loves talking about themselves, so if you want someone to engage with you and connect with you—there is no better way than to get them talking about themselves.

How to Find Anyone Interesting

Curiosity is a major driving motivator for me, and it's taken me years to realize that not everyone else feels the same. I've met plenty of people who don't care about other people's lives, their interpersonal dynamics, what they're doing, or where they're going. I get it, some people are just 'not interested.'

If that stance resonates with you, think about the fact that curiosity is an important trait of genius. Great minds like Claudia Jones, Albert Einstein, Ruth Lawrence, Richard Feynman—and my mom (who was a member of MENSA)—were all curious characters who asked great questions and found answers which changed the landscape of the world for all of us. Curiosity keeps your mind on its toes. Instead of passively listening or accepting what you're told, you engage, ask questions, look at things in different ways … and that strengthens the muscle that is your mind. Curiosity also opens up different possibilities, because instead of accepting things as they are, you'll want to delve deeper. Seeing beyond the expected leads to uncovering cool things in your life. If you choose to be curious, you'll quickly see that people are fascinating—but sometimes you just have to do some digging.

A friend who is a terrific conversationalist once told me that he goes into every conversation assuming that the other person is very interesting—so he makes it his job to figure out why and how. If he's bored with the conversation, he takes it as a sign that he needs to ask better questions. (It should come as no surprise that everyone who meets him thinks he's very interesting.)

How to Uncover the Interesting Human Underneath

Whether you're chatting with someone online in a breakout room or out in the real world—how can you find them interesting? What kinds of questions should you ask? Here are ideas to get your mind rolling in the high-speed curiosity lane:

1. **Find common ground**

   While finding something in common might seem like the most obvious way forward with someone you don't know, it can be even more connective when that commonality is established around something that's uncommon. Maybe you both are obsessed with those mesmerizing sand cutting videos on Instagram, Norwegian death metal, unsolved murder podcasts, or maybe you each have biblical-like knowledge of the Simpsons and can toss around your favorite Groundskeeper Willie deep cuts. Of course, if you don't want to open with, "I'm in the middle of a fascinating dive into Esther Perel," you can run with, "What's the best podcast you've listened to this month?" Or "Is there a show you love to quote?" "Is there anything surprising in your musical genre rotation?"

2. **Dig into the why's**

   In the process of conversing, you've learned this stranger breeds Corgis, the Queen of England's preferred breed. You really aren't into Corgis but digging into why the stranger like Corgis so much may lead the conversation down some interesting paths. If you can bond over something they're passionate about, this is a great conversational avenue.

3. **Get the 'How did they …'**

   Find out how they became interested in something or got so good at something. Asking "Is there a story behind that?"

is a great way to ask someone about something interesting they are wearing. It's also a great follow-up question when people make random declarations. For instance, if someone says, "I love martinis," asking if there's a story behind why they love them, or where they first tried one, may take the conversation somewhere interesting.

4. **What's the best or worst?**

   When I'm struggling in a conversation, or there is an awkward lull, I'm a big fan of asking people for their 'best and worsts.' Could be what was the best and worst thing that happened today, this week, or this year. Or it could be much more specific like what was the best or worst thing they've ever eaten, seen, etc.

5. **Better questions ... better answers**

   I'm mindful that sometimes when conversations aren't feeling as inspiring as they could be, that I'm to blame because I'm being too passive in my question asking. A better question will always get you a more interesting, detailed answer. For instance: "What's the most fun thing you did this summer?" compared to "What do you do for fun?" Humans are typically forgetful—I know I am—so the more prompts the better.

Connect First, Work Second

Approaching anyone with the mindset of how they can advance your career, help you get season Yankees tickets, or introduce you to anyone—is ill advised. No one wants to feel used, manipulated, or like they're a stepping stone to someone or something else.

Focus on connecting to everyone as people first. Everything else—like your work or life goal—is secondary. What I mean by this is, even if you're at a party at the Fancy Food Conference, talking about work isn't going to build a solid human connection. You want to connect as humans. The fastest way to do that is to get to know the person you're chatting with on a fundamental human level. You can start by asking open-ended questions that encourage your new friend to tell you their stories. For instance, asking how they got into their field of business, is a much more engaging question than asking how long they've been at their company. Beyond the here and now, I find everyone has a dream they're inspired by. As I mentioned before, back when I was a financial reporter for Institutional Investor, a well-regarded New York City company, my job was talking to high powered real estate investment bankers at top companies like Morgan Stanley and Goldman Sachs. I would often meet my sources out for a drink, but I rarely ever talked shop with them. Instead, I'd ask about their families, their upbringings, what they did on weekends. I never met one who didn't want to quit Wall Street and write a book, a screenplay, open a gallery, or shoot a movie. They were all in the rat race for the cash and had hopes of escaping one day. Did not talking about work hurt me? Not at all. I had the highest number of cover stories of any reporter on my team, because when I reached out to my sources they wanted to help me, and would often give me scoops I could go chase down!

Initiate Meaningful Conversations

When we're first meeting someone, we typically ask, "So, where are you from?" Then we ask about work. And sure, it'll probably get people talking, but I want to encourage you to connect with people in more unusual and practical ways. Sometimes it can be as simple as asking a question that would resonate with you at that moment. For instance, if you've just been fighting with traffic you could ask the person you're hoping to connect with, "Does it feel like traffic is beating you up more than usual lately? Or is that just me?" Or maybe you're dealing with the fact your eight-year-old child is on a losing streak on the soccer field, and you'd love some advice: "This is random, but what advice would you give to a parent who is suffering every time their kid's soccer team loses?"

These types of questions seem unexpected, but they are incredibly vulnerable. You're sharing something personal about your life and where you're at right now with a stranger, creating an easy opening for connection. The 'out of the blue' aspect will hopefully give your exchange a sense of novelty and charm. It will also help you be more memorable because you didn't ask, "Do you come here often?"

If you want to be even more random, try to ask things that will get the other person laughing. Why? Because laughter is the golden connector.

- "How long would you last in a zombie apocalypse?"
- "Who is your celebrity crush? I'm really having a tough time deciding between Jamie Dornan and Idris Elba."
- "You look great. Did you get lots of sleep last night?" (This is very funny when you don't know the person you're addressing.)
- "Hi I'm (Name). Let's skip the chitchat and discuss the important issues. Do you enjoy pineapple on your pizza?"
- "What's the best thing about today so far for you? 'Cause I'm loving this cool breeze."

Once the person is laughing and responding, now it's your turn to build on anything they share with you. If these types of questions don't resonate with you, there is no harm in going with something a tad more expected, but still connective. For example:

- "How do you like to spend your free time?"
- "What's the most interesting thing you've heard or listened to lately?"
- "If you could go anywhere in the world, where would you go?"
- "What's something most people don't know about you?"
- "What skill do you most wish you had?"
- "Got any irrational fears? I'm scared of …"
- "If we played the six degrees game, are you connected to anyone interesting? Famous? Newsworthy?"

Everyone likes talking about themselves, and they really love talking about themselves when they know they have a rapt audience (remember that Harvard study I mentioned?). Well, they'll enjoy it even more if they feel you're truly interested and engaged. Next chance you get, lean in and get your listening ears on!

Listening Is Everything

I'll go into more details about how anyone can be a great listener in Chapter Six, but I wanted to share an interesting assignment a friend suggested to me. He and I felt we struggled with talking too much at social events, because we're both big personalities, so he came up with a game for us to play.

While we both have lots of great ideas, advice, and wisdom to share with people, he suggested that we would be more likable and engaging if we gave ourselves one hour at specific social events in which we couldn't contradict anyone, couldn't offer advice, and could only add supportive complementary dialogue. If we weren't doing those things, we had to strictly be listening to everyone around us. I thought it was an interesting idea because it forced me to really look at the way I was engaging with the world around me, and it encouraged me to zero in on all the positive things being discussed.

At the next event I was invited to, I gave it a shot. Initially I struggled because it felt like I was muzzled, and I mentally wrestled with the idea that I wasn't supposed to talk. But then I realized it was a matter of slowing down and processing what I could and should share, so that I followed the rules. The slowing down forced me to listen more, and that created a feeling of balance in my conversations. At events that followed, I slowly tried to embrace the approach more and more as I noticed that the people I was talking to softened when they felt more heard and when they got to speak more than their fair share! I think positive social fallout is well worth having to listen to everyone a little more.

The ideal conversation should be a total give and take, with each person speaking about half the time. That means staying quiet half the time, which can be really hard for many of us. Dr. Marty Nemko, a career coach and NPR radio show host, talks about a traffic-light strategy that can help us monitor our chat style:

- You get a green light for the first twenty seconds you are talking. Your listener is liking you, as long as your statement is relevant to the conversation and hopefully in service of the other person.
- If you go over that first twenty seconds, you get a yellow light for the next twenty seconds. Now the risk is increasing that the other person is beginning to lose

interest or think you're long-winded.

- At the forty-second mark—your light goes red. Yes, there's an occasional time you want to run that red light and keep talking, but the vast majority of the time, you'd better stop, or you're in danger.

Have A Killer Story Handy

What's your best story? You know, the one you love to tell—and are great at telling? Having an amazing story locked and loaded in your conversational arsenal can be a powerful connective tool. Even better if the story involves humorous or outlandish plot twists like being tossed into a foreign jail cell with a drunk, a one-eyed man, and a hooker. Stories showcase your unique personality but also give your listener an instant sense of who you are and how you interact with the world.

Great stories don't have to be very long or even all that crazy. You could just tell the story about how you once ran for a plane, and when you got to the gate, the attendant had JUST shut the door. Undeterred, you dropped to your knees and started frantically making the praying gesture through the window to the pilot who was sitting in the cockpit—directly in front of you. Of course, with that kind of behavior you magically got on that last flight to Ottawa out of JFK that day!

It's helpful if you have a story that has a little bit of surprise in it. Makes everyone laugh, and say, "Wow!" Or look at you like you're the most interesting/inspiring/awesome person they've ever met. Still not sure what I mean?

LET ME TELL YOU A STORY:

I was once sitting in a bar in downtown Ottawa, Canada, working on my laptop in the middle of the day. Billy, the bartender, seemed very charming and we struck up a conversation that meandered around until we got on the subject of our favorite places to go. Turns out his favorite place in the whole world was Panama City. I was a little surprised at that, as Panama City seemed kinda random, but what did I know? I'd never been. Billy kept talking about how much he loved it there, so I started taking notes about what he loved there and got his email just in case I ever made my way in that direction. Oddly enough, about six months later, in late August, I wanted to go on a week-long vacation, and Panama City was calling my name. I emailed Billy, and he was nice enough to put me in touch with one of his dear friends who lived down there.

A few weeks later, when my boyfriend and I landed in Panama, we had already lined up a welcome cocktail with Billy's bestie 'VJ'. Not only did VJ live in Panama City, but he turned out to be a Panamanian Senator who also happened to be a lead singer in a band and a TV celebrity. VJ was an engaging man with a booming personality, who had launched a TV show called Your Lucky Day! in which the lucky winner of that episode was awarded cash, and the viewers watched how the winner spent their money. The show was a massive hit in the mid-2000s, and VJ was extremely well known. To go from chatting in a bar in Ottawa to having drinks with a Panamanian celebrity senator was pretty crazy. But that was only the beginning of this hilarious tale.

VJ and his lovely wife Daniella were attending a family wedding the following Friday, which was going to be our last day in town as we were flying off to Boca Del Toro in North East Panama early Saturday morning. This lovely couple suggested we should crash the wedding as it would be a fantastic night to remember. Initially we were hesitant, but the more we thought about it, the more we realized we were being silly not to attend this glittering affair, even if we didn't have the right attire for something that was likely going to be very glamorous. The morning of the wedding, we decided to drive an hour and cross Panama to check out some of the beaches on the other side of the narrow country. We had a great day snorkeling, swimming, and eating amazing fresh seafood. Around two o'clock we decided to head back to the capital city, so we'd have time to nap and get ready for our fancy wedding crashing. However, on the drive back, military guards—armed to the teeth—waved us over to the side of the dirt road. The leader leaned into our car and asked us to produce our passports which we didn't have as we'd left them in the hotel safe. Thinking that being pulled over and asked for ID was highly unusual, I assumed this was just a play for a 'special road toll'. Road tolls in Central America are pretty common. You can often see two police officers holding a chain across a road forcing cars to stop and drop a donation into their handy bucket. Maybe this was a road toll, or maybe it wasn't—I wasn't sure but either way the guy with all the machine guns strapped to his body, who seemed to be in charge, understood me perfectly well when I told my partner we needed to, "Find some money to pay them off." At the notion of impropriety, he got very worked up, and told us to pull up further into an area well off the road, where I noted there was some sort of official looking building. From there he led us, without our phones or personal belongings, to the little building which turned out to be their jail, complete with holding cells. Mr. Machine Gun firmly told us to sit down and stay put.

It was the middle of the afternoon and we had to be back in Panama at 8:30 pm to attend the wedding reception—so I was obviously nervous and worried. Plus, it was an odd scene in the jail. Next to me was a woman, who was dressed like a lady of the evening, an older man with one arm, and another American who seemed to have been drinking for four days straight. Nonetheless, I figured that in an hour or so, once the Captain had calmed down, they would release us and we'd be on our way. We hadn't done anything wrong! But an hour went by. Then two. My partner started to get extremely nervous and agitated until he finally insisted that I needed to do something. I asked the guard if I could get my phone out of the car. Much to my surprise he didn't have any objections. While I didn't want to bug VJ, because I knew he was getting ready for his family member's wedding, I didn't feel like I had a choice. So, despite having met him only once … I texted him and asked if he could possibly talk these morally upstanding military men into letting us go. He texted me back almost immediately: Sure, what's the number there?

Next thing you know, the main phone rings in the hut, and the desk officer answers it. He looks excited by the call and rushes out to hand Captain Machine Gun the receiver. The Captain takes the call just outside the hut, and we hear him going on and on in Spanish about how we suggested he might want a bribe, and how this was totally unacceptable. The call seemed to last forever before the Captain walked back in and handed me the phone. VJ was on the line waiting to talk to me and he was quick to scold me for the whole situation. I was extremely apologetic for having insulted the Panamanian military, and I apologized profusely to VJ. I could tell he was smiling when I finished, and he told me he was looking forward to seeing me later at the party.

I handed the phone back to the Captain and apologized again. He held the phone for a minute while staring at me. Then he asked: "How do you know VJ?" to which I replied as we got up and headed for the door, "Through a Canadian bartender."

Commit to being curious about everyone you meet, and you'll be well on your way to being one of the most interesting people in any room. Enjoy figuring out what makes everyone interesting, fascinating, and unique, and you'll walk away the party hero.

What's the Point?

The key to being a captivating guest is taking an interest in others. Get everyone talking about themselves and you'll have a million admirers, and a very packed party schedule.

4

Tiny Connections Will ... Get You a Better Job

If your current job is leaving you cold, it's likely time to think about what's next for you. Maybe it's time to pivot into a new industry, get promoted out of your current group, or change companies and go work somewhere that's got more WOW factor. No matter what you're thinking, it's time to ask yourself who has the power to hire you into the role you want. Do you know anyone who does that type of hiring? If yes, then plan to take them for lunch to pick their brain about how to 'next-level' things at work. If no, it's time to map out a plan for how you will meet this type of person, befriend them, and dazzle them with your wit, charm, and perfectly suited work experience. While you can hit meet-ups, attend online or offline networking events, and comb through online forums and LinkedIn—there is one sure-fire way to move you to the front of the line, and that's moving forward with the help of someone on the inside.

From the outside, it can seem like everyone BUT YOU is independently figuring life out for themselves, but that's unrealistic. Most people are relying on their network of family, friends, and co-workers to navigate everything from getting a raise to buying their first home, proposing to their partners, or even managing the care of an aging parent. Barbara Streisand wasn't wrong when she sang about people needing people, because life is a lot easier when someone can show you the ropes. So if you don't have an 'in' wherever it is that you want to go, it's time to get a mentor.

Mentor Up

Getting a mentor is a great way forward. Typically, a mentor is someone who is well connected, or has five, ten, or even twenty-five years more experience than you—so they really know their way around the industry you're interested in. That said, their qualifications aren't all that important, but their street smarts, accomplishment roster, and long list of connections will make all the difference. Having a mentor is like strapping a booster pack to your CV (curriculum vitae or resume).

When it comes to gaining access to desirable companies, your mentor may know someone on the inside, or their extended connections might. When it comes to helping you brainstorm and outline your path forward, they can offer valuable advice because they've been there, and they've likely coached and supported other people on their assent. Looking to pivot into another industry, a mentor can make email introductions, or they may go the extra mile and suggest an outing (lunch, golf, or group drinks, etc.) so influential folks can meet you, like you, and want to hire you!

Eighty-five percent of jobs are filled because someone knew someone who helped that person get the job.[28] The trick is not meeting as many people as possible, it's knowing a few well-connected people who can vouch for you and are willing to refer you to a few other well-connected people. Plus, when you think about the fact that 70-80 percent of jobs are never advertised, it makes very little sense to be doing deep dives into job sites, and much more sense trying to meet influencers.

Not sure how to find a mentor or how to approach them? The internet has plenty of in-depth guidance. In a nutshell, you must know what you're trying to accomplish. Identify who you look up to. Do your research and comb through your existing network to see who might be a good match. If no one fits the bill, ask your network for introductions. Know what you're going to say before you reach out, because a carefully crafted elevator pitch can help support them seeing the value in mentoring you.

You'll also find it beneficial to craft your mentor-mentee relationship, so you make it easy for your potential mentor to want to say, "Yes." Maybe you converse for 30 minutes every two weeks on Thursday mornings before work? Or you meet for a power walk around a park once a month? Whatever you both decide, you'll want to maximize your time with them, so always bring your questions, and prepare to soak up their wisdom.

Don't Discount Strangers

Just because you don't know someone well, it doesn't mean they won't try to help you. It's all in the approach. I've written to different people in different fields, in hopes they could give me pointers or make introductions for me. Sometimes they respond, sometimes they don't. That's life. But I think it's always worth a shot. That said, when it comes to reaching out to strangers don't get discouraged easily, and don't take a lack of response personally. When I catch myself getting frustrated, I remind myself I DO NOT KNOW THEM. I don't know their life. I don't know what they're going through. They may have a sick child, relationship issues, or they may just be buried under hundreds of emails. Plus—they don't know me, so they don't have a lot of impetus to respond. That said, I typically:

1. Reach out via email or LinkedIn

   Wait a few days

2. Reach out on another platform like Twitter, Behance, Instagram

   Wait a few days

3. Figure out their work phone number, and leave them a voice mail, then follow that up with another email that communicates something along the lines of: *Just touching base as I would still love to connect.*

This approach is very persistent and may seem a bit over the top, but if you do it in a slow, gentle but direct way, the person will understand that you are not going to go away until they have acknowledged or responded to you. This is a classic salesperson's approach, or you could say it's the ol' 'squeaky wheel gets the grease' approach.

If you've just read this and your stomach knotted up in a ball because that sounds so uncomfortable and hard, I hear you. It is uncomfortable and hard. Connecting with people we don't know is challenging work that requires skill, forethought, kindness, and care. It requires courage. Courage to be rejected and ignored. That's when you just have to keep reminding yourself: it's not personal, and they don't know me. Then you must move on and figure out who else can help you achieve your goals.

Where Can You Meet Influential Folks?

Influential people are busy and focused. They tend to have routines, private clubs, high-end gyms, and preferred restaurants and entertainment venues. So, it's your job to think about where those spots may be in your area then start frequenting them.

Can't afford the money for a private club membership? Start asking everyone you know if they know any members. Then you're going to beg that person to take you on occasion. You living your best life, with a great job is a great cause, so be transparent and upfront with them. Tell them you're looking to move out of food service and into tech, and you want to meet more influencers in that world. Tell them exactly who you want to meet. Having them on your team can help because now you've got them thinking about ways to support you, plus they may already know someone and can facilitate a quick introduction.

As for gyms, restaurants, and fancy entertainment venues, you don't need to pay the dues, eat there regularly, or buy lots of show tickets. Instead take specific classes at that gym (core strength, boxing, or spin classes) so you can try to connect around the water cooler at the juice bar, or in the locker rooms. Can't swing paying for fancy meals in top restaurants? Hang at the bar (just drink fancy water and tip big) in hopes that someone interesting sits down and you get talking. You should always hit the bars near the entertainment venue on the nights there are big events, to see who you can run into. Be brave, go alone, and give yourself a set amount of time before you slink out. When we go alone, we are forced to engage with the bartenders, the waitstaff and more importantly everyone around us, and you never know who might know someone who can help you. Obviously, I'm assuming you're making the effort to stay off your cellphone in this scenario, because the goal is connection. While others around you may be on their cellphones, if you catch their eye and smile, you might be able to start up a conversation. It's certainly worth a shot.

LET ME TELL YOU A STORY:

I was fascinated by real estate investment, and in 2001 when the stock market collapsed after the dot com bubble, I was certain there was an easy and smart way to buy real estate with syndication investments from many people. But I didn't have an MBA and I didn't have a track record. How could I even think of starting a company that would buy large multi-family investment properties?

Insecurities running rampant, I realized I needed a mentor inside the structured investment real estate world. Initially I wasn't hopeful; I went to art school, and most of my friends and coworkers were all liberal arts or marketing majors. Nonetheless, I got invited to a real estate luncheon the Princeton Club was hosting in midtown Manhattan. I don't remember how I scored that invite, but I do remember going alone, walking in late and realizing I was probably one of 10 women in a room of 150 men. It was intimidating for sure. Once the speaker was done, and the room broke to mingle and graze at the lunch buffet, I ended up chatting with a charming older gent named John. Within five minutes, this insightful human asked me, "What are you doing here Jennifer? What is it you're hoping to find?" Without missing a beat, I said, "I need a real estate mentor."

With a twinkle in his eye, John looked at me and told me he knew just the guy I had to meet. He was the CEO of one of New York City's most esteemed Real Estate Investment Trusts (REIT), and worked directly for one of the most well-respected real estate investors in the United States, if not the world. John promised to set up an introduction for me, and he made good on his word.

Two weeks later, I was sitting in an office overlooking Park Avenue talking to Jeff about my hopes, dreams, and investment syndication plans. His background was wildly different from mine. Fancy MBA, years at the top investment banks, and now running his own $100+ million REIT. I struggled with how he could help me. Maybe I'd overshot the mark. But over the course of several meetings and the occasional phone call, he would share his thoughts on the world of real estate investment, and I often walked away from our talks inspired, calmed, or more secure in the path I was taking. I worked very hard to meet Jeff, but I have often wondered how I would ever have met him if not for John's introduction. Our worlds were so totally different.

When in Doubt … Play Sports

That said, had I played polo, I would certainly have run into Jeff. Polo, or the sport of kings as it's called, is a huge draw for the rich, powerful, and famous. People who play polo want to connect with others who are passionate about the sport, and of course they want to celebrate their wins. If you're looking to connect with the type of person who's into polo, it's a great idea to get involved. If you aren't able to play the game (requires owning polo ponies and being able to ride horses — a pretty steep barrier to entry), then start by reading sports news, following the schedule, attending matches, and trying to score invites to any of the parties. (I'm a huge fan of party crashing, and rarely consider an invitation a requirement. Instead, I do my best to ferret out the where and the when, and I insert myself.)

Don't actually want to play a sport? Don't stress. Find a way to support tournaments. Volunteer to help the organizers. Do whatever it takes to get you mingling with the participants, so you can connect, pitch yourself, and hopefully turn a casual connection into your next great job. One dear friend of mine, James, has been playing golf since he was a teenager. He's so good at it, people literally throw real estate deals at him in hopes that he'll play more golf with them. Seems having a scratch golfer (one who can shoot par on pretty much any course) is a real asset, and it works out well for him. He loves to play golf, have a few beers in the clubhouse after, and if he picks up a real estate deal in the process … even better.

After knowing James for over a decade and listening to his stories, it is my firm opinion that people who play golf are especially prone to being able to connect their way forward into better jobs and better opportunities. Other sports that attract powerful, smart, connected humans who can help evolve your career include tennis, racquetball, cycling, hockey, sailing, squash, high-end car racing, as well as pick-up soccer and football leagues in affluent suburbs. Playing sports with the people you aspire to emulate aligns with the idea you have to 'dress for the job you want—not the job you have.'

Plan Your Next Move

Armed with a mentor, or leveraging the help of others, it's time to put your plan into action. If you're looking to get into a new industry, your next steps are very different than if you're trying to rise through the ranks or get a new job in your current field somewhere a whole lot cooler.

LET ME TELL YOU A STORY:

Jana was an incredibly successful physical therapist at the tender age of 31, but she was overworked and utterly burned out. After a horrific personal tragedy shook her and her family to their core, Jana took a hard look at her life in New York City and at all the stress she was soaking in … then decided to chuck everything. She walked away from her mortgage, her booming practice, and dove headfirst into a year-long trip around the world that included traveling to 22 countries.

She jumped out of planes, kayaked Fjords, climbed Kilimanjaro in Africa, and started building up an Instagram following as she was doing all this. (Hey, who doesn't love watching intrepid young women doing awesome things? #LivingMyBestLife.)

Working with a life and career coach, she started figuring out what was next for her and she really started to dream big. She had no idea what she wanted to do but she knew she needed guidance and mentorship. She worked here and there, leveraging her training, but stayed focused on jumping from amazing experience to amazing experience around the globe. One minute she was hanging in Morocco with celebrities, and the next she was attending the well-regarded Summit Series in Utah. How did she manage it? She leveraged her connections to move herself around the world, getting invited to one thing after the next.

Her world traveling could be the whole story, but it's not. The interesting twist came when one of her Instagram followers, Maria, with whom she'd developed a rapport, reached out and suggested that they meet up when she was back in New York. Over coffee, Maria suggested Jana meet her coach Jonathan, because it sounded like their paths were thoroughly aligned. The only issue was Jonathan lived in Ojai, California and Jana had no plans to head that way.

Fast forward a few months, and what do you know? Jana is in California passing through Ojai. In an odd twist of fate, she gets extremely ill with a freak infection and is taken to the hospital. Suddenly she's an inpatient for days and who is the only person she knows in Ojai? You guessed it: Jonathan.

She reaches out and connects and the next thing you know he not only shows up but spends every day engaging her in meaningful conversation. They talked about what it means to be human, and discussed frameworks they wanted to create that would support their purpose and their vision for helping others. Talk turned into action and they decided to host a talk at Burning Man, the powerful gathering of minds in the Nevada

Desert that happens around Labor Day. A few months after that, they gave another talk at a focused gathering that supports elevated leadership. In just two months, they'd gone from casually throwing down a workshop to sharing their work all over the world. Jonathan and Jana manifested a nine-month timeline in just two months. Years later? They are not only still very connected, but they are still passionate about working together and are both based in sunny California.

LET ME TELL YOU ANOTHER STORY:

In the east village of New York City is Cooper Union, a well-respected art school. While Julia was a senior at 'Cooper' as it's called—she was a resident advisor in the school's dorms, which is how she met Liz, a Cooper junior. The two young women bonded over art, design, and all things New York, so it was only natural that Julia thought of Liz when she heard about an amazing internship opportunity at a boutique Soho design agency. (Julia was working in the school's admin office and had too much on her plate to consider the job for herself!) As luck and talent would have it, Liz applied and got the desirable paid internship. After a year working at this well-known boutique agency, Liz got a better offer from another agency so she introduced Julia to the Boutique design shop to take over her responsibilities.

Life in New York can be busy, so it's no surprise that the two women lost touch. However just a few years later, they randomly ended up working at the renowned advertising agency Kirshenbaum & Bond, where they reconnected and rekindled their friendship. After a few months, Liz was again offered a better opportunity at the hottest fashion company back then: Lloyd & Co. At that time, Lloyd & Co. had all of the Conde Nast brands such as Vogue, GQ, Vanity Fair, along with other well-known brands like Smart Water, so it was a great place to get on your resume. While there, Liz referred Julia to the HR department, and they brought her in as well, so they were again working together. How did they get so tight? Why did they follow each other around from company to company? Julia credits the nature of advertising and the fourteen-to-sixteen-hour days that the young staff members put in. She and her co-

workers would work from ten in the morning to eleven at night, then go out and blow off steam in New York City bars and clubs. She would do this seven days a week, because everyone in advertising in Manhattan is always working ... especially when they're under thirty-five.

Breaking into a new industry:
This will require you revamping your resume and LinkedIn profile in order to align more with the position you'd like to nail down in the new industry. If you're in food service (working as a waiter for example) and you want to get into pharmaceutical sales, you have to use language that resonates with hiring managers on a sales team, like 'close rate, projections, or CPM (cost per thousand).' Identify someone who has the job you want and enlist them to mentor you through the process of transforming your external face, then work with them to get a sense of how you could best position yourself to get the job you've identified. This may come down to someone giving you a shot because they hope you'll work your tail off. Or someone believing that your past experience is an asset. For instance, you might have excellent customer service skills which are universally important in all sales roles.

Getting a promotion:
If you're looking to step things up and get promoted, it's critical to know who has the power to make that happen for you. Is it your hiring manager? HR? The company's CFO? Who assigns titles, reworks job descriptions, and gives pay increases? Sometimes it's more than one person. The fastest way to figure it out is to ask your supervisor, "I am ready to take on more responsibility and be promoted. I'd like to sit down with you to make an action plan, so I know what I need to do to make that happen in the next three months." If they aren't the right person, they'll most likely tell you who you need to connect with, so you can sync up and start putting your plan into action. Every person you work with is an ally when

you're climbing the corporate ladder, so be sure to remember that. The more people like and respect you at work, the more likely you will be put forward for promotions. Even the front desk receptionist could have a say, so make sure you're kind and professional with everyone (which, of course, you should be anyway).

Get a job somewhere cool:

When it comes to getting hired anywhere that has a high cool-factor score like Apple, Instagram, Tesla, Google, Spotify, or Samsung—the game becomes almost uniquely about who you know. Ninety percent of those jobs are placed through friends, coworkers, or connections. To get into one of those organizations, you're going to really have to up your game, and you're really going to have to be the bomb!

Do you know anyone that works at the company now?

- If yes, start taking them out, and getting to know them really well. They are likely going to be your primary inroad. (And if you do get the job because of them, make sure you give them gifts, take them for an amazing dinner, or send them an insane bouquet of something they'll like. Your gratitude won't be forgotten!)
- If no, then go through LinkedIn, and see who you know that does know someone there. It's time to set up some group drinks, etc. If no one you know knows anyone at the company, you're going to have to get creative. Find out which bars the company employees frequent after work. The receptionist might tell you if you can get her on the phone, or you might be able to see where employees go by following their Instagram accounts.

Think about how you could meet and befriend just one influential person at the company and make that your goal for the next month. LinkedIn will give you a lot of intel, for example some employees list their pick-up soccer leagues. It's time to watch some games. Other employees might note they are patrons of a specific museum. It's time to start going to openings. Turn meeting connectors into a bit of a game, and you might realize you're having fun trying to get that new job.

Next Stop A Better Job

A friend once told me that getting a new job was proving way too time consuming, and she was close to giving up because she couldn't manage the searching, networking, and following up—on top of her current job. While I understand how she felt, at the end of the day, it's important to keep your eye on the prize. Most likely your new job will be more rewarding, possibly come with a bigger paycheck or better culture and nicer perks. Whatever the advantages, it's likely going to affect your life in a positive way, so going the extra mile to make the connections will all seem very worthwhile.

What's the Point?

Knowing the right people is the one surefire way to getting a better job. Doesn't matter if you met on the tennis court or in a bar—when the right person tells HR to get you an interview … it happens!

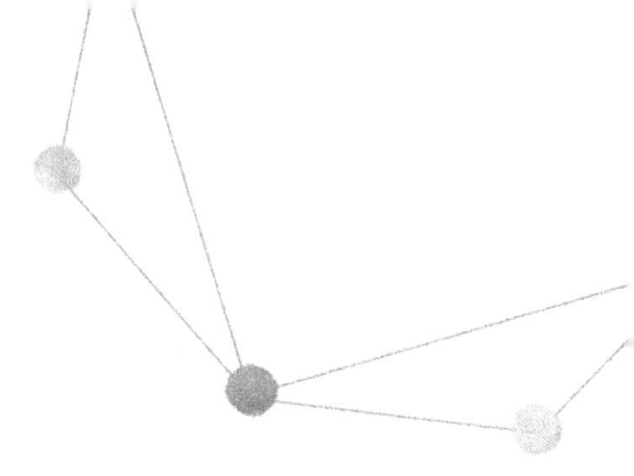

5

Tiny Connections Will ... Get You Laid

While writing this book about life-changing connections, I found I was avoiding the topic of flirting. I'm not sure why, because flirting can be a vital social process that freely doles out confidence and self-esteem. Flirting is one of the amazing ways we get others to believe more truly in their own attractiveness, both psychological and physical.

When it comes from a place of kindness and creative excitement, flirting is a non-physical gift we give another person that isn't meant to manipulate them. Instead, it honors all the fabulous juiciness that is their being. Sure, flirting can mean you're ready to throw down and do the sheet mambo, but it doesn't always have to mean that. Sometimes flirting is simply a charming exchange between two humans who appreciate each other. When you examine the basics of a platonic flirt, a good exchange has to convince each person of two things that are at odds with each other:

A) this person would love to sleep with you

B) this person would not sleep with you; but for reasons that have nothing to do with your shortcomings

No small feat really, when you think about the possibility of hurt feelings.

So why was I avoiding talking about these amazing social connection mechanics? At first, I wondered if maybe it was too obvious? Then I wondered if I felt it was too sexualized a subject for me to want to touch. (Sorry, I couldn't resist that pun.) When I dug deeper, I think I was avoiding the judgment I might attract if I laid 'the flirt motives' bare. Absolutely, people flirt to connect sexually with others, but that's not the only driver, and I bristle at how simplistic most people's view of this social exchange can be. Flirting is one of the fundamental ways humans interact with each other. It's a time-honored way to signal attraction, interest, and mutual awareness. It's really a silent language spoken by people around the world, one that requires many skills. It requires intellect, creativity, empathy, and an understanding of body language. At its best, flirting can be an art, whether the flirter is manipulating a potential customer, being playful, or looking for a soul mate.

When we flirt, we're signaling our interest in others in tiny increments, which enables both parties to gauge each other's interest in each other. Flirting is driven by instinct and emotions, rather than by logical thought—so powerful information is conveyed. How those are received determines how things go down. You never know when things will or won't click.

LET ME TELL YOU A STORY:

When I was in my early thirties, after having been in advertising and marketing for almost a decade, I got myself a paid apprenticeship with a real estate mogul that owned a 116-unit property out in Pottstown,

Pennsylvania, which was about two hours from Manhattan where I was living at the time. (Pottstown is a very rural small town that's about forty-five minutes northwest of Philadelphia.) To get this glorified internship, I bought a car (something that's utterly terrifying to most people from New York City), and took a massive pay cut. Lucky for me, the new gig included a free two-bedroom unit on the property I was going to be managing, so I didn't have to drive back to my Manhattan apartment all the time.

In a matter of weeks, I went from working on Madison Avenue for clients like Apple, Adobe, and IBM, where I was writing and presenting million-dollar ad campaigns—to living in Pottstown where I spent my days learning how a property management office was run. Well, if it had been run back in 1975! It turns out that Pierre, the owner and my boss, didn't like digital anything—so all the leases were typed by hand on typewriters, the rent ledgers were kept in binders and written in pencil, and the tenants were hand-delivered notices on a weekly basis. To be honest, I wasn't sure what I was doing there, but I was determined to stick it out for five or six months, or until I had enough courage to buy some real estate for myself. My goal was to start owning passive income properties so that I could stop worrying about how I would make money later in life, as advertising and marketing typically don't hire many women over the age of forty. (It's a young person's industry, and most ad agencies are run by aging men. Not women. Hopefully this will change.)

When you work in advertising in New York, you typically work from ten in the morning to around eight or nine at night. Suddenly, I was working from nine to five every day, and I now had all this time on my hands at night. I got a gym membership—but that only fulfills you so much—so I was also watching DVDs from Netflix—back before they became a streaming service. (This was 2004!)

One night after work, I decided that instead of going to the gym, I would really mix things up and ride my bike to the video store to get the next DVD in the series I was watching. (Shout out to the cast and crew of

Nip Tuck.) Well, when I got my bike out of storage, the tires were flat. I asked my neighbors for a bike pump with no success. That left me pushing my clunky, retro looking bike down the highway next to the townhouses. Next, I tried the 7-Eleven but still no luck. I have no idea why I didn't give up and go home, but instead I kept walking alongside this rinky-dink two-lane highway, hoping that someone along the way would have an air compressor. Lucky for me, I hit pay dirt just a few minutes later when I pushed my bike into a garage that looked like it hadn't quite closed for the night. I could see a mechanic working on a car in one of the bays.

This particular summer evening, I was dressed in a white T-shirt, white shorts and even had on white running shoes. As I pushed my bike up to the tall, rugged mechanic, the sun was streaming all around behind me, blinding the poor guy. I asked him, "Do you have air?" to which he responded, "I sell tires." I figured he wasn't that bright, and repeated myself, "That's nice, but do you have air?" He laughed and thought I was light in my loafers, cause clearly if you sold tires, you had compressed air as well. Without another word, he grabbed my bike, pumped up my tires, fixed a few things that were amiss with the bike, and asked me where I worked.

We talked about biking and rollerblading, and as I walked away moments later, I knew I would be hearing from him in the future. Despite the fact that no information had been exchanged beyond my place of work, I had a solid feeling I'd see him again. Sure enough, he sent his brother into my real estate office to grab a brochure and take a tour, and not long after he called the office and asked me out. In a few short weeks, we started dating and quickly became real estate investors, and life partners for the next thirteen years. Later when he told the story of how we met, he would tell people that he thought an angel had walked up, because I was dressed all in white and with the sun streaming all around me I had a radiant holy glow. Kismet? Destiny? Who knows? Either way, that random encounter shaped the rest of my life, because not only did I get the courage to jump into real estate with him by my side, but I'm also blessed to call the two bonus kids he brought into my life part of my closest family.

Chemistry

Talking to someone is one of the easiest ways to connect. But how do you take it up a notch, so that you both feel that little something extra? A spark? Chemistry? So you both feel like you've clicked? Turns out that when it comes to sparking chemistry through conversation, your choice of topic, tone, pacing, and body language are all critical.[29]

Stay Neutral

If you're looking to connect in a way that's going to green light some sexy time, you're going to want to keep your topic of conversation pleasant. Which typically means keeping it neutral. Asking about family, kids, hobbies, and their latest adventures will likely work out well. Listening to someone gush about the ski trip they just took to Utah, or how their son just got a new job at IBM, can help build the bonds you need to take things to the next level. You can also refer to some of the fun conversation starters on page 55, which will keep your listener amused and engaged.

Tone, Pacing, and Body Language

Beyond topics that feel comfortable, you'll want to be mindful of how your tone, pace, body language, facial expressions, and emotions are impacting your partner. Slowing down how quickly you speak can convey warmth and magnetism. Smiling can add a lot to the moment as well. Have you ever said something, then said it again with a smile? Same sentence, but it sounds totally different! Smiling is an easy way to lay your cards on the table so the other person knows exactly where you're hoping things will go—and is encouraged to want to go there with you.

Looking the other person in the eyes is also important, as it conveys how intent you are on listening to them, hearing them, and really connecting with them. When someone is distracted—

maybe playing with their phone—it can really leave the other person feeling cold. No one wants to play second fiddle to technology. When you are leaning into the conversation with your body, that can also send clear signals. A light touch on their arm or shoulder as you deliver a punchline will clearly convey your attraction.

Getting to Click

Author Ori Brafman believes that one of the tricks to making a click happen is sharing vulnerability. You have to expose a weakness and hope the other person reciprocates. Maybe you lost a pet whom you miss terribly, and the other person has had a similar experience? Or Brafman suggests you can ask authentically connective questions like, "What's something meaningful that's happened to you in the last week?" Or, "Who are you feeling closest to in your family right now?" so you lay down the pathways for a really great 'click.' While Brafman makes a great point, I can't imagine asking those questions unless I was three cocktails deep. Even then, I'm pretty sure whomever I was chatting up might run for the hills. A better question might be: "What's the worst moment from your week? I'll share mine if you share yours." You might think this is a lot of work for a roll in the hay, but I'm hopeful that your pick-up ends up that much better, that much more fun BECAUSE you really connected with the person beforehand. Maybe you can be someone's best part of the week!

Flirting for Courtship & Sex

So much of this book is about maximizing random moments and capitalizing on the sizzle you feel while connecting with another human being. Rarely is that sizzle more electric than in a sexually charged exchange. While flirting can be very exciting, it can also be terrifying. Everyone is scared of rejection and it's often top of mind when we're out of our element. No one likes being shot down. Fear of rejection is largely why most flirting is very subtle, and is done using eye contact, tone, and playful mannerisms. Sadly, it's so subtle, I think many of us miss the hints we should be picking up on. I can't tell you how many times I've been told that someone was flirting with me and I hadn't noticed at all. Here are the core tenants of flirting:

- Frequent eye contact
- Smiles and laughter
- Playful manner
- Complimentary approach

Here are my favorite "You're interesting … Appealing … Hot … Wanna strike up a conversation?" approaches:

Hold A Gaze

Where you are doesn't matter for the following exercise, as it works just as well for people at bars or sitting across from each other on a plane. Start by staring at the other person while counting to three seconds. One, one-thousand. Two, one-thousand. Three, one-thousand. If they hold your gaze for all three seconds, ladies and gentlemen the game is on! If they don't hold your gaze, it's possible that they don't dig your vibe, or maybe they're a little shy. For greater insight, I suggest waiting a few minutes then trying to catch their eye again and repeating the whole exercise. Four seconds later, hopefully you're both still looking at each other and grinning wildly. Next step will be a verbal exchange that will solidify your interest in each other, or they may open their mouth and kill the whole vibe. You never know.

Pay Them A Compliment

Since flirting is the recognition of your attractiveness—paying someone a compliment seems like an obvious way forward.

Try to make the compliment sincere and hone in on something you genuinely noticed and appreciated. Maybe their eyes are a unique shade of brown, or you're into shoes, and you noticed theirs were particularly cool. Maybe you love quality fabrics, and their coat is clearly excellent quality alpaca. The more personal and unique the compliment the better.

Be Suggestive

Once you're getting positive cues from the other person, why not be verbally playful and suggestive? For instance, if the object of your flirt is telling you a story about how they went swimming, or dancing, you might respond, "I bet you're something to watch when you're glistening in the water." Or, "I would love to take you dancing next week, if that would be fun for you." You could have been cruder and responded, "I would love to see you all sweaty," but by keeping the conversation elevated and less base, you can keep the dance going. (And that initial dance is one of the best parts of the flirt!)

Touch

Initially, it's best to avoid touching people you don't know. They may be responding to your flirtation because they appreciate you, enjoy the dance, and/or don't want to hurt your feelings. To further gauge the situation, you can look them directly in the eyes and hold their hand a little longer when you shake hands. Gently put your hand on their shoulder, when you excuse yourself to go to the restroom. Touch their forearm in conversation, ever so casually. Seeing how they respond to these subtle but telling signals will give you more intel.

Flirting to Underscore Feelings for Your Partner

We all need reminders about what is charming, attractive, and exciting about ourselves. To be reminded of what attracted us to our mates in the first place, and why we're staying with them.

You might touch their arm while at dinner. They might take your hand while you're crossing the street. Maybe you always greet each other with passionate kisses and compliment each other's appearance regularly. The little flirtatious gestures between a couple can do more to support their long-term care for each other than a random bouquet of flowers or perfunctory, scheduled intercourse. These gestures cement and reinforce that you find your partner attractive, interesting, and that you want them to know you're feeling for them deeply—mind, body, and soul.

Flirting to Get What You Want

It's absolutely true that flirting greases the wheels when it comes to facilitating any kind of transaction. Maybe you want a car upgrade at the rental counter. Extra hotsauce for your wings. Or maybe you want help getting your luggage to the hotel room and free WIFI. It really doesn't matter what you're trying to achieve, a little light flirting can make any transaction feel more charming and personal.

I'm not suggesting anything lewd or sexualized, I'm suggesting that keeping a friendly, playful, focused, and engaged tone can go a long way to support the other person wanting to help you out. I often approach the whole exchange by putting myself in the other person's shoes. If they're stuck behind a security desk, maybe I bring them a hot coffee because they can't get one. Maybe I travel with individually wrapped candies, chocolates, or Hershey Kisses, so that I can offer everyone something BEFORE I ask them to assist me with whatever my needs might be. This has never worked in terms of getting me upgraded on a flight, but I did get an extra 30,000 travel miles from the Quantas team on a Christmas Day flight to Sydney after I gave the crew gifts and a holiday card. It wasn't the business class upgrade I was shooting for, but nonetheless my gesture made their day a little more special and made them feel a little more important.

The core to flirting for what you want is understanding that everyone is human and fundamentally wants to be appreciated, cared for, and taken into consideration.

Flirting—You Still Got It!

When someone flirts with you, it can be a huge boost to your self-esteem. It typically feels great and can make you feel alive and electric. When someone flirts with us out of the blue, it can ignite a renewed sense of joy and appreciation for ourselves and for others. It can rekindle memories and physical sensations in our bodies that remind us of our innate vigor, of a time when responsibilities didn't weigh so heavily or maybe it just reminds us that we really like—or liked—sex!

Flirting and having someone flirt back with you can inspire people to change their minds and bodies. It can inspire you to stay healthier, so you feel attractive and physically desirable for as long as possible. It can inspire you to read more and watch less TV, because you want to bring your most intellectual side to the forefront.

Taking care of our physical appearance—be it updating our wardrobe or getting a gym membership—is an easy way to let the world know we're still very much aware of our own vitality. When we see older women in four-inch heels, rocking cocktail dresses, and men over fifty in slim cut dress shirts and jeans with cutting edge footwear—we understand immediately the value they place on being seen as thriving.

Flirting Just Because …

Flirting 'just because' is some of the best flirting around. You're not doing it to get anything, and it doesn't need to amount to anything. You're doing it for the fun of the flirt. For the spark of the connection. It's flirting that encourages you and others to share more of one's true self in the random in-between moments. Those times when you might be sitting and waiting for your friends in a restaurant, so you start chatting vibrantly with your waiter. Or the moments you're waiting for your Uber, so you strike up a charming conversation with the bellhop who is standing nearby. Passing the time by enthusiastically engaging with people is not only great practice for staying present and in the moment, but you never know where those conversations will take you. Maybe the bellhop knows a great little jazz club, and you end up having a much better night as a result. Or the guy behind the counter at a local convenience store suggests a great little BBQ place for dinner. Perhaps your waiter suggests an excellent cocktail lounge for your after-dinner adventures. The pleasure of conversation alone will make your day better. We both feel seen and heard as humans, not solely as service providers, customers, or clients. Looking past people's roles in life and seeing their juicy, awesome, sweet centers is a treat that we should indulge in as often as we can.

The art of getting you laid more is really very straightforward. It's the art of connecting. The art of being truly engaged and interested in someone else. Sure, you might be doing it for pretty focused reasons, but if you're honest, forthright, direct, and kind—I don't think there is anything wrong with that. You'll notice I didn't say lie your way into someone's bed by telling them what they want to hear. Be direct, honest, and upfront. Because at the end of the day, the person will appreciate having all the facts and knowing where you're coming from.

Plus, who knows, maybe you're totally on the same page and your connection will really grow as a result.

What's the Point?

When you want to play with others: PLAY BIG. Show up in the highest and best way you can muster. Look deep in their eyes, and level with them about where you're at and what you want. There is nothing shameful about sharing real, intimate pleasure with another person when you're both on the same page.

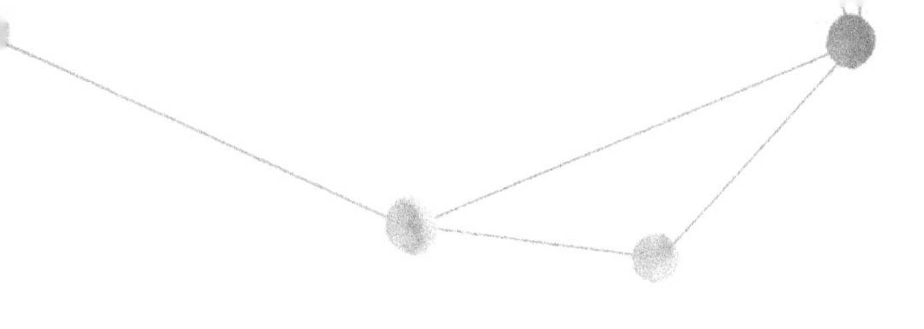

6

Tiny Connections Will ... Make You a Better Person

I have gone many times to Burning Man,[30] the week-long free-form radically creative experiment that's held annually in the Nevada desert. I feel that most people would benefit from living their lives in more alignment with the ten guiding principles that Burning Man established for all attendees. Some of these principles include: radical inclusion, self-reliance, self-expression, civic responsibility, and my favorites—participation and leave no trace. These names sound a little airy-fairy, but once you've lived them you see just how important they are for shaping the kind of world we all want to live in. These ideologies not only make the world a better place, but when embraced, they make us better people. People that others will search out and enjoy more—and that's a great person to be. Let's check out a few of these principles in more depth, so you can get a better sense of why I think these Burning Man principles are so supportive when it comes to being an awesome human.

Radical Inclusion

This is the idea that anyone can play, do, or be part of whatever it is you're mixing up. With regards to Burning Man (BM), I know plenty of people who assume it's an event primarily for very rich tech entrepreneurs or super-hippies. Not the case. Through the BM low-income ticket program, the organization strives to be inclusive because they want lots of different people at the event. They want different points of view, creative styles, and musical expressions. People with different personalities and backgrounds who will show up and make this year's 'burn' (as the BM attendees or 'burners' call it) as unique, interesting, and exciting as the years before. BM has realized that if you only hang with a few types of people, only listen to one kind of music, or watch one kind of movie—your world becomes monotone. If we could all strive for being this inclusive in our personal lives, imagine the impact.

Radical Self-Reliance

Radical self-reliance means that you bring everything you need to have a great time. So, if you're going to a party, a good citizen will bring what they want to drink. So that means you don't just bring one beer knowing full well you'll drink three, it means you bring the three you'll drink and an extra offering for the party gods. It's like packing a kazoo on a camping trip—a little bonus for everyone involved. Bring what you need, and a little extra to make everyone else's time that much better. Imagine what every party would be like if everyone showed up with that kind of attitude?

Radical Self-Expression

This concept is about sharing your gifts with the world. Whatever those gifts may be, it's on you to bring them and share them. If they stay buried in the back drawer of your psyche, where's the fun in that? With a doctrine like this, it's no surprise that BM is overflowing with a boatload of creative expression. From extravagant art projects and fascinating TedX type workshops, to amazing costumes, accessories, and outlandishly themed camps—everyone is encouraged to express themselves boldly. The outcome? Much laughter, enjoyment, curiosity, emotion, vulnerability, and above all—connection. When you really show up, people really see you. How amazing is that?

Participation

Ask yourself: How amazing would it be if every person at work, or in your friend group, was an active participant? How cool would it be if everywhere you went, everyone participated eagerly, really showed up, and regularly asked each other, "What do you need?" Or "This is how you can help." Burning Man has fostered a culture that encourages everyone being as engaged as possible. When you see massive six story high art installations in the middle of a desert, you know many hands were involved because—it truly takes a village. Yes, Burning Man is extreme. Yes, it seems radical. But in order to get everyone to see and feel a shift, the non-profit organization had to be structured around participation principles that push us well past our normal comfort zones, so that all attendees can feel a shift, transformation, and a real sense of community connectedness.

If I had to distill these BM principles into something a little more understandable, I would tell people that in life it's critical to:

> **Show up:** Don't stay home and ride this one out. The meeting, lunch, party, or baptism won't be as good without you in the mix.

Ensure everyone around you is having a better time because you are there: Working with others to create, build, or envision something that's bigger than the sum of its parts will have a lasting impact on you and those around you. Plus, that kind of behavior often makes great stories!

Participate: Don't be a universal dead weight by 'sitting this one out'. Get involved in whatever is happening. Offer to help with whatever needs to be done. Your participation can make things run faster, better, smoother, or make whatever it is just that much more fun and interesting.

Make others feel seen and heard: Help people feel like they matter.

Allow yourself to be seen: Show up and be yourself—warts and bruises included.

Share: Give of yourself, your time, your effort, your personality, your perspective.

Being a good citizen of the world is so much more than spectating, which is why living these principles can be life changing. Life is action. It requires work. While I know we all have a tendency to be effort avoidant, if we want closer friends, better jobs, more interesting vacations, we can't afford to live like that.

Everyone Wants to Matter

Some people are perfectly comfortable to kick back and watch life go by, while others want to jump into the thick of things. But no matter your approach to life and living, every soul on this earth wants to believe that they matter deeply. There are lots of ways to feel like you matter such as raising a family, doing work that's meaningful, or volunteering. Other ways to feel like you matter might include paying someone an unexpected compliment, offering a helping hand, or simply letting someone cry on your shoulder.

Being seen and understood is the centerpiece of feeling like a human that's living on earth and having an impact. You may not be Ariana Huffington or Greta Thunberg but having the people around 'get' you, goes a long way toward feeling like you matter ... and everyone wants to know they matter.

Make Others Feel Seen and Heard

When you take the time to connect with people and make them feel seen and heard, you're in essence making them feel more valuable, more engaged, more connected, and certainly less alone. Plus, if you're doing it in a full-hearted and sincere way, you'll experience the same kind of validating feelings. It's a total win-win! When we put in the effort to make someone feel like it matters that they are there, wherever 'there' may be, and that it matters to you how they are doing—it can be one of the greatest gifts in the world for you and for them. Here are a few ways you can make new acquaintances, and even old friends, feel more connected to you.

Practice engaged listening

There are some easy ways you can make your conversation partner feel like you're fully present. For starters, put your phone away, or at least flip it so it's face down, and notifications won't shift your concentration. If you're not in a work setting, but you're near a laptop, you might find it helpful to tilt your screen away from you— so you're not even tempted to glance at it. If you can't move your screen, move your chair so your body is lined up facing whoever is speaking. These types of subtle gestures indicate that the other person has your full attention and is your priority.

Next, it's time to get fully engaged, and practice what's often called 'active listening' which in essence means you engage all your senses and really hone in on what's being shared. You can do this by:

- Keeping eye contact, smiling, leaning in or nodding as they speak—so they know you're present
- Asking good questions
- Keeping an open mind and doing your best to be non-judgmental
- Being patient – if they pause while they're speaking don't rush to jump in
- Paraphrasing what you're hearing back to them, this is a good way to gain clarity and to help the other person feel heard
- Asking for clarification when necessary

When we listen in this manner, we're going to get a better sense of where the other person is coming from, and we'll earn the other person's trust. If you're doing it well, they'll feel supported, encouraged, and you may even help them see things in a different light when you ask thoughtful questions.

Below is an example of active listening:

Lorie: Hey Jess, I'm sorry to be a downer, but I just had a fight with my brother and we haven't spoken since. I don't feel great about the situation, and I would love to talk to someone about it.
Jess: Talk to me, I've got time. Can you tell me a little more?
Lorie: It's silly but I'm so upset. We were fighting about what to do for my sister Marie's birthday.

Jess: Oh man. I can see why you're upset if you're not speaking now.
Lorie: Yes! My brother infuriates me. He assumed I would plan a whole big bash, and I'm swamped right now. He just thought I was making excuses and didn't want to participate.
Jess: That's tough. How did that make you feel?
Lorie: Upset. Really mad. And I probably feel guilty that he had all these plans and it felt like I was a roadblock. I broke down and told him to manage without me, but that doesn't feel good either.
Jess: You have a lot on your plate right now. I can imagine having a little time to sort things out would be helpful.
Lorie: Yeah, you're probably right. I really appreciate your listening.

Appear Open-Minded

Trying not to set any judgments or form preconceived notions about people before you really know people, is SUPER HARD. My antidote? When I catch myself making up stories in my head about anyone I don't know, I get curious. Does their outfit strike me as unusual? I ask them about it. Do they have an unusual accent? I ask them about that. As humans, we often want to put people in different boxes and label them because it makes us more comfortable. We have a tendency not to appreciate undefined people because they are at odds with what we think we know.

People are one of the greatest gateways to opportunities. When you accept one another, which can be rare these days, you open a door instead of closing it with judgment.

Pay More Attention

Most of us are so busy living our lives, we often can't make time to truly take in our environments, or really process what's going on with the people around us. We're listening to music or podcasts while walking, driving, or doing almost anything else, and we're reading our devices pretty much everywhere—doesn't matter if it's the bathroom stalls at work or the elevator of our apartment building. We are not paying attention to the world around us. Ask yourself:

- Would you notice if one of your coworkers was wearing the same clothes two days in a row?
- Do you know how the people you see regularly (work or social) take their coffee or tea?
- Has someone gained or lost weight recently? Or maybe cut their hair or shaved off their beard? You might not want to comment but being observant is an important connector for people.
- Does someone not look as happy as normal? Maybe today is a good day to connect with them more deeply than you do normally.

These are just a few ideas to get you aware of how perceptive you are. Most of us don't want to change our day-to-day habits because they are comfortable. So perhaps challenge yourself to notice the shoes in the stall next to you in the bathroom, or the faces of the people in the elevator or on the bus. Give yourself a daily ten-minute challenge to just be present and look around at the world. You might be surprised by where that leads.

"I define connection as the energy that exists between people when they feel seen, heard, and valued; when they can give and receive without judgment; and when they derive sustenance and strength from the relationship."
— Brené Brown, Author & Shame Expert

Practice Radical Thoughtfulness

When we spark joy in other people, it makes connecting with them a lot easier. Think about it, when someone does something kind for you, or unexpected, it's so lovely it can make us melt a little on the inside. It makes perfect sense that you can make people's days a million times better by doing small acts of radical thoughtfulness, ramping up thoughtfulness to a level that's just not expected. The easiest way to do this is to put yourself in other people's shoes. Ask yourself: What's going on in their day that you have the power to improve?

Here are a few radically thoughtful ideas:

- Bring someone a cup of tea from the nearby deli, diner, or restaurant. And of course, you get it just the way they like it because you've asked them, "How do you take your tea?" (I do this for my building security guards because I know they can't leave their post.)
- Tidy up after yourself at home or at work. The people around you will sincerely appreciate it, and you'd be surprised how many points you can get for making the bed, emptying the dishwasher, folding the laundry, etc.
- Ask the gate attendant as you check-in for your flight how their day is going, and take a sincere interest in their response because you know full well that no one else ever asks. (We're typically much too focused on having our own travel needs met to give them a second thought.)
- Call an elderly member of your community when you're at the store just to ask if they need anything on the fly.
- Send thank you cards whenever possible. The more

time we spend in gratitude, the more aware we are of what there is to be grateful for all around us. Postable makes it so easy too—you log on, write a note then THEY mail it and send it out. Check it out: postable.com/partner/jennash

- Offer to take notes for a co-worker if they're going to miss an important work call.
- Offer to help someone with their luggage or groceries, when it's clear they are struggling.

Doing things to make other people's lives a little more enjoyable may seem like a small thing, but it can really improve their willingness to connect with you. I can't tell you how surprised airline counter employees are when I offer them individually wrapped chocolate kisses and try to make THEIR day better. Or when I say thank you in Arabic to the cab driver as I'm exiting because I'd correctly figured out he was from Algeria. When we pay attention to the people around us, a whole world of magical connections can open up. But we have to be present and engaged to witness it, and when you're actively thinking about how you can make someone's day a little better, I don't think you could possibly be more engaged.

Share Yourself Generously

People can feel seen and heard when they feel safe. People tend to feel safe when they feel they can be vulnerable with you, which is facilitated by you being vulnerable with them. You can do this by sharing your feelings, your opinions, your fears—in other words by leveling with each other. While this may feel challenging when you've just met someone, it's often easier than you realize. People often confide very personal things to strangers, because they're less concerned about feeling judged, or they feel more comfortable sharing something awkward with someone who doesn't know them. People sitting next to each other in an airport lounge can easily end up talking about all sorts of personal things because there is an unspoken awareness that you may never see each other again. There is an implied safety in that anonymity. If you are talking to someone who is struggling to manage the illness of a loved one, and you've been there—don't hold back. Tell them about your experience. It can create a very strong, memorable connection.

Openness & Vulnerability

Paul recently went through a terrible divorce. His ex fought him every step of the way, and the whole thing was super hard on their kids. However, he never reached out and shared what he was going through with his friends, so when he announced he was getting a divorce and was moving to a different state, everyone was pretty shocked. No one had a clue, and they certainly didn't know how to support him in that 'surprise' moment. Paul hadn't wanted to burden his friends with all the drama he was going through, but then was surprised by the lack of empathy he felt from his friends. He realized over the next few months that his friends were hurt that he hadn't confided in them. That he hadn't wanted to share what he was going through. Those friends would have wanted an opportunity to be there for him and support him through this rough patch while he wanted to be strong and stoic and show he could get through it alone.

I think we can see both sides of this right? No one wants to let their guard down, and be seen as weak or vulnerable. Yet in those moments when we do, we are actually being so strong.

Brené Brown, author and research professor at the University of Houston, tells a story about her daughter Ellen's third grade classroom marble jar. Ellen's teacher had a marble jar where she added, and subtracted marbles as needed to track the classroom's behavioral progress. If the kids made great choices together, the teacher added marbles to the jar. If the class made poor choices, the teacher took marbles out. When the marble jar was full, the class would have a celebration which was something everyone looked forward to.

One day, Ellen came home from school and slumped to the floor crying. When prompted, she explained, "I will never trust anyone again." Brené Brown's first thought was "Damn right!" because she wanted to protect her kid. But as she asked more questions, it turned out that the whole class had laughed at her daughter, to the point where the teacher had removed marbles from the jar—trying to get everyone to behave better. While Brené doesn't share exactly what happened, it really doesn't matter. Because she goes on to explain to Ellen that trust is like a marble jar: You share the hard stories and hard experiences that are happening to you with friends. Friends whose marble jar you've filled up. Because over time, they've done thing after thing to underscore that they can be trusted with your emotions, your thoughts, and your actions. The marbles in the jar give both of you a sense of comfort and security and help solidify your friendship and care for each other.

We let the people in our lives in, so they can support and care for us. When we open up like that, we're supporting deeper, more loving connections. Being vulnerable shows our friends, and family that we trust them. Our lives are not social media perfect, and we're letting them see the soft, real, and very vulnerable underbelly that is our real life. Plus, when we are vulnerable, we are leaving the door wide open for others around us to be vulnerable with us.

I've had friends who have dealt with panic attacks or insomnia for years in silence, and never opened up to me. The minute I went through a rough patch in my life and mentioned I was dealing with these same types of issues—they started confiding in me, and our friendship deepened.

If you struggle to open up and be vulnerable with the people you care about, take time to reflect on why you feel compelled to be 'so strong' and to protect yourself from their love and support. Do some self-analysis, and take steps toward connecting more deeply with yourself. When you do, you'll give the gift of being a more loving, courageous, and connected friend to all the people in your life.

Struggle with Openness & Vulnerability? Practice on Strangers

Want to share something dark from your past? Confess concerns around uncomfortable issues? Who better to do that with than someone you'll likely never see again? Mario Smalls is the author of the book, *Someone to Talk To,* which is based on in-depth interviews with graduate students coping with self-doubt, stress, health care issues, fear of failure, poverty, and other similar issues.

Smalls found that when people had uncomfortable things they wanted to talk about, most people didn't turn to their friends and family with whom they had strong ties, instead his test subjects took great pains to avoid sharing whatever it was with close friends and family. Why? Because these relationships were both complex and fraught with expectations. Instead, more than half the time, they chose to confide in people with whom they had weaker ties, as the need for understanding or empathy trumped their fear of misplaced trust. Typically, Small's test subjects would find themselves confiding in the person sitting next to them in the waiting room at the doctor's office. Or someone at their hair salon. Interesting right?

This makes perfect sense to me, because I often think people will go out of their way to listen to, support, or help people they don't know. We don't have the same judgments in place for strangers that we have for friends and family. A friend and I were recently talking about why some people didn't seem to support their loved ones' business initiatives the way strangers did. She said, "Friends and family are less likely to help when it comes to supporting my entrepreneurial ventures. I think they prefer not to get involved and ruin the relationship. Or maybe they don't believe in me? Or they just don't have enough faith that I can succeed? Either way, it's easier for them to stay removed than engage."

The takeaway is that while talking to strangers may seem stressful, it can actually be a relief because there are little to no expectations. Most people assume that a conversation with someone random will just be a blip on their radar. So, it's something you can approach easily, and if you end up having a total mind meld—well, count yourself lucky.

The Power of Sharing

"Friends share all things," said Pythagoras of Samos, the ancient Ionian Greek philosopher. While he probably meant it literally, given that he and his adherents led a monastic lifestyle in which they shared everything from ideas to food and piss pots, I think we can extrapolate that when we share our ideas, our wisdom, our possessions, and our friends, we live richer lives for it. Got lots of ideas? Share them. Know lots of stuff? Share the wealth. Own lots of houses? Why not let your friends and family enjoy them when you're not there … or when you are there. This is by no means a popular concept as we typically spend a lot of time and mental energy marking our territories, in fear that people will take what's ours and use it for their gain. While I admit people do occasionally steal ideas and even belongings … in reality it's a pretty unlikely outcome. Most people are too principled, busy, or lazy to be bothered stealing from you. So why not live life open-hearted? More comes from this approach in my experience. Plus, when others see the example you're setting, they may be inspired to follow suit, and you'll benefit from their ideas, emotions, vacation homes, and from a deeper connection.

Share Your Ideas

If you're working on an idea, share it, talk about it, allow others to contribute so they can evolve the concept. You might be surprised to find that they help you see your idea from different angles. Some people think that everyone will steal their ideas, so when they are working on a new project, they refuse to talk about it. They're very secretive. They really try to keep things close to the vest. While I understand that approach, I don't believe that's the best way forward. It's closed off. It's disconnected.

Share Your Knowledge

I love helping other people if I can easily support their vision with my skill set. I am passionate about traveling, food, art, culture, health and wellness, real estate, property management, and the hospitality industry—as well as more highly focused topics like helping women overcome their discomfort around money, tailored support for college grads, and helping companies support remote workers. If I've learned something that will benefit someone, I'm quick to share the insight. If I can suggest great restaurants, a great podiatrist, a great pizza dough recipe, or a trick for getting blackberry stains out—I offer it up as appropriate. I want my knowledge to support all those around me.

Share Your Resources

I travel a lot and if no one is in my apartment while I'm gone, I have historically had no problems letting friends crash. I would hope that the same courtesy would be extended to me, and I often remind myself it's all 'only stuff.' I have a friend who drove a sexy black Porsche 911. As a New Yorker, I didn't often get a chance to drive anyone's car, let alone one that nice. While we were out for a long weekend in the Hamptons, the lush green area on Long Island that's just a few hours outside of Manhattan, he offered to lend me his car so I could run a quick errand. As he tossed me the keys, he simply said, "Don't ride the clutch!" I did a double-take, assuming that surely, he had more instructions than that as he lent me his six-figure four-wheeled baby. Nope. Not him. His approach to material possessions was very simple. Remember they were just things. I very much appreciated that perspective.

Sometimes resources are intellectual property, for example you can visit my website:

www.jennash.com

to download connection blueprints, and cheat sheets that will support you turning small interactions into something amazing.

Share Your Connections

I think one of the best things in life is being able to connect with others—in fact, I've written an entire chapter about it in this book. Need a specific type of artist, therapist, contractor, musician, restaurant, bar, dentist, or maybe architect? If I can reach into my Mary Poppins style magic bag of connections and help you achieve, whatever you're trying to accomplish it's my honor and privilege to make that introduction. Being able to say, "I know just the person!" or "I've got the perfect place for you" rocks. I simply adore helping people get their needs met, and it gives me a deep sense of satisfaction to do so.

This web of humans really can be extremely useful to myself and others so while I am happy to share, I do admit to doing so with a certain degree of awareness. I don't share willy-nilly with just anyone, as I like to really ensure that both people will benefit from the introduction. At the end of the day, it's not a win if only one party comes out ahead.

Share Your Skills

Know how to build, craft, grow, bake, or draw something? That's a skill many people could use. If you've got gifts, please, pretty please share them. Speaking as someone who had to beg a local green thumb to help me with my garden, the gift you're sharing can really change people's lives—or at least alleviate stress.

So where am I going with all this sharing? When you share anything from your connections to your gifts or resources, you have the opportunity to create powerful connections that people deeply appreciate.

What's the Point?

Dare to be the person who really shows up. Dare to care more by asking everyone how they are doing. Offer assistance. Listen really closely. Share your full self with abandon—because that person is awesome.

7

Tiny Connections ... Can Earn You More Money

Getting a better job is one thing. Making money from assets is something different. It's more fluid and flexible. There is plenty of moolah to be made beyond the confines of your nine to five. Your connections are the key to getting it. I've spent twenty years investing in real estate as a side hustle while I consulted full time for Fortune 100 companies, and I assure you that deals happen more frequently for those who are well connected. This is why throughout this book, I'm suggesting you angle your way into events where you can meet the type of people who have the ability to inspire and encourage you. If you need to network your way into a higher socio-economic group, then do that, because rubbing elbows with people who can't pay their rent isn't going to motivate you. When it comes to cash-making opportunities, it's all about who you know.

LET ME TELL YOU A STORY:

In 2002, I was single in New York City, so I answered a personal ad. An old-fashioned personal ad in the back of New York Magazine. That's how I ended up on a date at an Irish tavern with Pierre, a guy who was easily thirty-five years my senior. It wasn't going great. Pierre was very rude, and the date felt like a total waste of time.

The next morning, I was thinking about what we'd discussed and mulling the whole experience over in my head. Pierre had turned out to be a Harvard graduate who took great pride in the fact that he'd been running a successful commercial real estate business for many years. I wanted to get into real estate as well and was curious what wisdom he could impart. I couldn't help but wonder if meeting him had NOT been a waste of time, so I called him and owned the whole awkward situation, "Listen, I don't think either of us felt like yesterday's date went that well, but I am very interested in hearing more about your commercial real estate adventures. Would you be open to letting me buy you lunch, somewhere that's very convenient for you, as I'd like to pick your brain about real estate?"

He was flattered by the call, the way I was so direct, so he agreed to meet me for lunch in lovely Newark, New Jersey. Much to my surprise, the two of us were having a great lunch, and surprisingly getting along much better this time around. Pierre was impressed with my marketing experience, and over several weeks, offered me the opportunity to come work for him and learn the ropes of real estate management. A year or so later, I ended up taking him up on his offer and moved to a small town outside Philadelphia. A year after that, I purchased my first two real estate investment properties.

While this was a totally orchestrated meeting, I'm a huge believer that friends, introductions, and life-changing opportunities can cross your path at any time. The person who just hired you may become a mentor that supports your career for the next twenty years, or they could end up being the love of your life! No, I never got romantically involved with Pierre. Our age gap and his condescending attitude to everyone was just too much for me to overcome, but he did provide me with a much-needed push into the world of real estate ownership.

Everyone's an Expert

Some people collect art they hope will appreciate, while others sell their homemade jewelry on Etsy. It may seem like everyone's got a side hustle and they should, because most of us are hoping for a certain level of financial freedom before we're seventy. If you're looking for ways to make more money, one thing is certain: you know people who can help you, teach you, or motivate you. Every goal-oriented, driven person you know is working on a plan, and if you're lucky, they'll share it with you. By spending time with them, and asking good questions, you'll get access to a wealth of knowledge. They can tell you what has and hasn't worked for them, along with all the ins and outs of what they are doing. They can save you time by sharing their go-to resources; they can save you a headache by sharing the optimized approach they took three years to refine, or maybe they'll expand your thinking by sharing a perspective you never considered. Think about it this way: everyone has a window on the world. Everyone's window is a little bit different, so when you spend time connecting with people you are effectively spending time looking out their window with them. This vantage point can be extremely insightful and motivating. Plus, hang out long enough and who knows, maybe you'll be invited to join in on their next money-making adventure.

Retirement Planning

I am not a financial planner, but I do have friends who put hundreds of hours into managing their investment portfolios. They spend time on the phone with their accountants discussing different things they can do to minimize their tax implications, which means they know smart ways to save you money too. They may have strong ideas about Index Funds versus Target End Retirement Date funds—and because they've been doing the research for years, they are a fountain of knowledge.

Conversation Starters:

- "What are your top three tips? The tips you wish you'd been given when you were at my stage in the game."
- "Would you introduce me to your money manager?"
- "What's your management style? How often do you call your advisor or check on your portfolio?"
- "Any current tips you think I should know about?"
- "Can you give me three names of other people I can talk to?"

Taking investment advice from just about anyone is risky—so make sure you do your homework, and make a plan for taking advantage of this long-term financial approach.

Investing in the Stock Market

Have you ever noticed how two people who are really into the stock market may have totally different takes? One might be all in on stand-alone equities while another might be gung-ho on index funds. Each has done their research, each has solid data supporting their methodologies, and yet they don't agree. This means that as you move through life, you'll meet person after person who has a unique take on the subject at hand. If that subject is making their money grow, you're in for a lot of diverse conversations.

When you take the time to get curious about how people are

investing, trading, wheeling, and dealing—you are getting a valuable front row seat to different opportunities. A seat that has the potential to be measurably valuable—think zeros adding up in your bank account. Perhaps they attend entrepreneurial meet-ups, or they joined an investment club that you could join too. Think of it this way, one well-researched stock tip has the potential to radically change your holdings, and you never know who will have a good tip! A friend recently found out that her uncle Clayton was able to buy a Santa Cruz, California beach house thanks to a stock tip (buy Tesla) he got from his neighbor while they both were working on their lawns. Clayton's neighbor worked in finance, and Clayton trusted him so he took action that's paid many a sunny dividend.

Conversation Starters:

- "What kind of asset allocation are you using?"
- "How do you assess the risk of an investment?"
- "How do you decide when to get out of a holding?"
- "Do you have set return goals?"
- "What advice would you give to someone just starting out?"
- "Do you have any stocks you currently think are undervalued?"
- "Do you know of any investment clubs?"
- "Can you give me three names of other people I can talk to?"

Real Estate

Real estate is one way a lot of people make money. You can buy homes, renovate them, flip them, or rent them out. Or if residential real estate isn't your thing, you can buy, build, or renovate all sorts of investments ranging from multifamily and commercial to industrial properties. If you're not sure how to do this, it's time to connect with others who are doing it, or looking to get into it.

When I was first starting out in real estate, I asked everyone for advice. I wanted to know how they financed things, if they had a list of good mortgage brokers and what sorts of deal structures would work if I took on partners. I once went to a speed dating event, and while I was waiting for my round of speed dates to start, I struck up a conversation with a guy at the bar and told him I was desperate to get into real estate investing. He laughed and said all his besties were investing in real estate and I flat out asked if he would connect me. Sure enough, he introduced me to six guys who were all going gangbusters doing real estate deals. I called each one and talked to them about their approaches and got a sense of how it was working for them. One of them enjoyed chatting with me so much he suggested we grab a coffee and talk more. Turned out he was a tall, handsome guy, so while I didn't get lucky at the speed dating event, I ended up having several very fun dates with him and got lots of great real estate tips.

If you're looking to get included in real estate opportunities, start talking to everyone you know who's involved in real estate about what they're doing and how they are doing it. Someone might be looking for a partner or investor.

Conversation Starters:

- "What made you get into real estate?"
- "Where do you invest?"
- "How do you find your properties?"
- "What kind of deals do you do?"

- "How do you typically finance your purchases?"
- "Do you take investors in your deals?"
- "Can you give me three names of other people I can talk to?"

Entrepreneurial Opportunities

From launching a new Instagram cartoon account and growing the followers to over 30,000 in six months, to selling hats, jewelry, or jams online—plenty of people dream of launching their own business. Not only can this be helpful from a tax perspective, but the extra income is always appreciated. If you've been thinking about starting something and want some mentorship, or if you want to invest in someone else's start-up and become an angel investor—you're going to have to mingle with folks who are focused on their passion projects. If you're looking to start your own business, I would look to mingle with others doing just that. Anyone who's got a year or more of experience could be a great mentor.

If you're more interested in partnering with someone, and helping them grow their business, or an idea you both come up with—you'll want to network your tail off to find like-minded humans.

While I don't want to dissuade you from starting anything, it is worthwhile to note that 90% of start-ups fail. Why? Lots of reasons, ranging from there wasn't enough cash to fund the business, and not knowing enough about the vertical or industry, to crappy partnerships, bad research, or ineffective marketing.[31] Losing your own capital is one thing. It's quite another when someone else loses it for you, so definitely think about this and how you want to move forward with this money-making hustle.

Conversation Starters:

- "How did you get into (making specialty jams)?"
- "How do you distribute and sell (your jams)?"
- "How do you handle shipping? Do you do it in-house? Or do you have a deal with someone who is warehousing your product?"
- "How did you fund your business? Can you share any of those contacts?"
- "How is it going? Are you making any money? Or spending all the income on the business?"
- "How are you managing projections?"
- "Who does your books?"
- "Any interesting tax advantages you've learned?"
- "Can you give me three names of other people I can talk to?"

Making more money is absolutely all about who you know. In Chapter 4, which was all about getting a better job, I talked about how my friend James gets real estate deals because he's a scratch golfer, and people love to play with him. They will do anything to get in his good graces, including giving him real estate deals—sometimes for nothing.

Who you know matters. How you listen and interact with them makes all the difference. James happens to be one of the nicest humans I know, so I'm sure that beyond his expertise, his personality is helping things along. He isn't looking for money-making opportunities most days and yet they land in his lap because he's been invested in his community for thirty years, and is talented, smart, and well connected.

What's the Point?

If you're looking to make more money—look at the people around you. Spending time with others who are investing, flipping, or growing their wealth is key. They will inspire and encourage you.

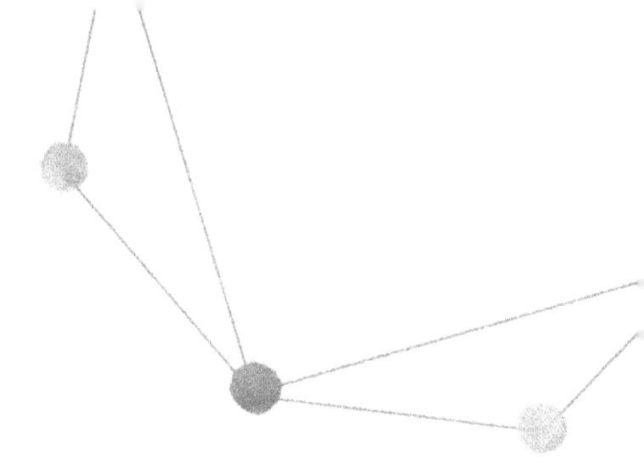

8

Tiny Connections Will ... Make Your Life More Exciting

No one wants to live in a movie where every day repeats on a loop. Days turn into months, months turn into years, all with limited opportunity for evolution, fun, excitement, or change. While we don't set out to live like this, it does seem that many of us do end up feeling like we've put our days on some sort of auto-repeat setting. We work. We eat. We see the same people. We go to the same places.

It might not suck, but could it be better? Abso-freaking-lutely.

Want to Live A More Exciting Life?

While you can change jobs, switch partners, move to a different apartment, take up new hobbies, or move to another city or country—sometimes those more extreme suggestions aren't practical, loving, or smart. Instead, one of the easiest ways to enhance your life is by adding new friends and acquaintances to the mix. Their new ideas, new opinions, insights, and past experiences will cast a different light on your world.

If we choose to hang out with people who are passionate about their lives, it's hard not to be influenced by their infectious enthusiasm and to feel inspired. If we hang out with smart people, we will likely learn a lot from them. If we hang out with people who are well connected, our circle of friends will also likely grow. While meeting new people you connect to on a deeper level isn't a given, it is deeply worthwhile. I'd go as far as to say that building connections is one of the few things you can do that's guaranteed to add value to your life.

Take a few moments and jot down what specific elements you feel are missing from your life. Wish you were more creative? More adventurous? Moved more? Were more engaged? These gaps can all be filled by connecting with new people—but first, you have to leave your house.

While this may seem like an obvious suggestion, sometimes having fun is more work than some people are willing to put in. Staying home, hanging with your friends and family is comfortable. Unfortunately, 'comfortable' is the enemy of the new, the fresh, and the creative. It's certainly the enemy of meeting new people who might just alter the course of your life. That doesn't mean you can't go to your favorite bar for the sixth Friday in a row, but it does mean that when your friends suggest a weekend rafting trip, that you consider going. That when your company asks if you'll give a presentation at a trade show, that you'll consider it, instead of just lamenting the loss of your Thursday evening. The choice is yours, and it always has been. You've got agency, baby. And you damn well better use it.

Say YES—and Then Take Action

So, what am I talking about when I say you've got agency? I'm talking about your personal power—the choices you make and the actions you take. More than anything, I'm talking about making the things you want to happen for you instead of waiting around for them to happen to you. Your life—the goals you achieve, the impact you have, the exciting things you do—is 100% under your control. It's all up to you. Things won't change if you choose to turn down the invitation, postpone the catch-up call, skip the event, or stick to the pre-planned itinerary. You have to say SUPER YES to unexpected opportunities

For example, I love to travel but worry that I'll miss out on some super amazing spots because I don't have my head buried in travel guides. The fear of missing out on the best cold brew in Seminyak and then reading about it later online, drives me nuts. (But not enough to become the kind of person that likes doing tons of research!) Instead, I often find myself asking random strangers on buses, planes, or ferries around the world, "What have you seen that you thought was amazing?" And, "What should I make sure to do?" The results never disappoint.

LET ME TELL YOU A STORY:

I was on a ferry boat in Koh Sam Mui, Thailand, brainstorming different things to do in Bangkok with a Dutch tourist who happened to be sitting next to me. He had some amazing ideas, and you can be sure I took notes, then took action. Days later, I was on a high-speed bike chase through the backstreets of Bangkok thanks to his suggestion that I do a city tour with Co van Kessel bike tours. The tour had me laughing like a hyena as we sped superhero-style down small back allies, trying to catch up to the main tour group. Most Co van Kessel bike tours are gentle affairs, but because we arrived late for our designated city bike tour, the head office had dispatched a nimble guide to zigzag us at a blistering pace through the alleys, all in hopes of catching the main tour. Little did that tour guide know, but that ten-minute high-speed catch-up was the best part of my week.

Not only did I take the stranger's suggestion about Bangkok bicycle adventures, but three weeks later, I was diving with majestic manta rays off the Komodo Islands in Indonesia based on his ideas for what to do in that region of the world. The gent on the boat had specifically suggested that the best way to swim with mantas (a lifelong dream of mine) was to get on a live-a-board boat from Labuan Bajo and dive around the nearby Indonesian islands. Manta rays have a wingspan that can easily reach ten to fifteen feet and are utterly amazing to watch as they easily remain perfectly motionless despite crazy currents all around. My scuba pod and I were clinging to rocks, fighting against the current to watch these gentle giants, while they didn't seem to be exerting any effort to hover above us! Diving with mantas is still one of my life's great highlights, and it never would've been possible if I hadn't—

Hold up for a second. How do you think I was about to end that sentence? That once-in-a-lifetime experience never would've been possible if I hadn't … struck up a conversation with that Dutch tourist? Is that what you expected me to say? Well, I'll give you partial credit since, yes, technically, I wouldn't have thought to add Labuan Bajo to my itinerary without his suggestion. But what made it possible? Me. I did that. Because I did something with the advice he gave me. I took action.

Yes: The Foundation of Improv Comedy

Years ago, I attended an improv comedy show. At the start of the night, the actors explained how the show worked and how they would regularly take direction and suggestions from the audience. They also explained that the foundation of improv was your ability to go with the flow. You always had to say "Yes" to whatever was being suggested, because if you said "No," the momentum of the narrative would come to a sudden halt. You could say "Yes and …" or "Yes but …" but you had to accept whatever was being proposed in the moment.

This principle applies very well to everyday life. It's important to be able to take action when life serves you up options and opportunities. You don't have to fully validate whatever is being offered, as you get the opportunity to evolve anything and make it work for you. So, if someone asks, "Do you want to go on a ten-mile hike on Sunday?"; you can say sure you'd love to, but you'd really prefer a four-mile hike. Could that work? Now you're having a conversation, as opposed to you having shot the idea down, and them feeling rejected!

Do Cool Shit, Meet Cool People

You know what a 'bucket list' is? It's a list of all the things you want to do on earth, before you 'kick the bucket' and die. Maybe you want to run a marathon, write a book, sing on Broadway, or maybe you just want to buy some land near a beach and build a super cool cabin. Whatever is on your list, here's what you might not know—you're more likely to do the things on your list when you're with other people who are down to do them too. Similarly, while you're out doing something cool, you're way more likely to meet cool people.

LET ME TELL YOU A STORY:

In 2016, my partner at the time and I were invited by some dear French friends to sail around Thailand for two weeks on a fifty-foot catamaran. While this might sound like a super fancy five-star vacation, it wasn't. Renting a boat in Thailand is much cheaper than almost anywhere else in the world, and we didn't have any crew except for a terribly amusing Russian skipper. Nonetheless, I was very excited about this opportunity, as I'd always wanted to spend time on a boat, and the prospect of spending Christmas floating around the Thai islands sounded incredible to me. Even without air conditioning!

One morning a week into the trip, we were moored off a small island where part of Leonardo DiCaprio's movie, The Beach had been filmed. Our boat captain had suggested that we take the sea kayaks and paddle into the island, through the cave-like entrance, because inside was a fantastically pristine beach. Since it was so early in the morning and no one else on our boat was awake, the two of us jumped in a kayak and paddled into the cave that led to the secret hidden island. We made our way into the very narrow cave that led to an open area surrounded by tall rock walls.

Halfway through the cave, I jumped off the kayak and swam with my mask and fins, weaving through the amazing stalactites and stalagmites. And in doing so, I noticed thousands of small fish in every direction that were dancing and swaying all around in a rhythmic pattern. It was amazing to watch, something I will never forget!

The little beach inside this island was very small, but we sat there for a moment and were surprised to see another couple come paddling up from the cave. How did they get there? We'd been the only boat moored at the mouth of the cave when we entered. The couple paddled in, and I told them to jump in the water to enjoy the amazing fish on their way out; they were excited at the prospect of seeing the fish, and on that note, we parted ways.

However, a few hours later, at a well-known snorkeling spot called Sail Rock, we saw their boat again. My guy was certain they were Americans, so after some friendly betting with our hosts, who were certain that this couple was French, my guy jumped into the water and swam over to their boat to strike up a quick conversation. He asked them if they'd seen the fish I had mentioned, and they talked about it before he swam back a few minutes later. He was happily triumphant as the couple and their daughter chartering the boat were from Seattle, Washington. We were surprised and delighted when ten minutes later, the couple in question—Maya, Blake, and their daughter, Alana—jumped on paddleboards and headed over to our boat.

Our new friend, Maya was even carrying a bottle of champagne to share with our boat. I remember I laughed when I saw that bottle in her hand because we had been going to Burning Man for a few years by then, and people often show up randomly at each other's camps with bottles of bubbles. It turns out Maya and Blake also loved Burning Man, and as we chatted more, we quickly realized we had a lot in common. As luck would have it, a week later we all had plans to be in Bangkok for a night. Naturally, we exchanged information and made plans to hit the town to get to know each other better. A week later, we had a great time running around Bangkok at night, and several months later, Maya and Blake invited us to go skiing with their family in their amazing Ski-in Ski-out home in Park City, Utah. Then, just a few years later, this lovely couple flew into New York to surprise me for an amazing birthday dinner, and we've continued to grow our friendship every year.

While I thought I was on a glorious two-week sailing trip around Thailand, I was, in fact, on a life-long friend-making adventure! Because I was open-minded, playful, and welcoming, this little plot twist became an amazing friendship.

Don't Overthink It

Saying yes to something that sounds like a bad idea is always scary but it often turns into a great story, and a serious bonding moment. It could be something as nuts as saying yes to the guy who takes you on a date bungee jumping off the Brooklyn Bridge at 2 am (true story) or volunteering every week at the nearby church, where they need help preparing and delivering meals for all the local shut-ins (also a true story). Doing things that are beyond your comfort zone can not only shake things up for you, but give you a new perspective on what's fun, important, or meaningful. Volunteering often reframes our lives and gives us a greater sense of sincere gratitude.

If you're unsure about what to do to shake things up, grab a friend and get brainstorming. Race car driving and jumping out of planes may be your ticket to a weekly adrenaline rush, or working in a wild animal rescue shelter with injured birds of prey might light you up on the inside. When we light up, we cast a glow around us, and everyone else is likely to see things a little differently too.

Surprise and Delight *Yourself*

And finally, there are a million ways to make your life more exciting that don't require a trans-Atlantic flight and a cat sitter.

For most of us, there are very few surprises that we can look forward to. Surprises seem to be a thing for children, something our parents and family members gifted us at a young age. But once we were young adults and all grown up, where did all the surprises go? Pregnancy and the sex of your child is one of the last real surprise holdouts, but with technology and gender reveal parties we even rush that along.

That said, humans come in all sorts of shapes, sizes, and styles. You never know what you're going to get because the outside rarely depicts the inside. I've met punk rockers who were the sweetest teddy bears, and unassuming-looking suburban moms who would tear you to shreds if you took their parking space. There is something utterly delightful and surprising about not knowing who you might meet on your outings, adventures, travels, or while you're in line at the movie theater. That kind of unexpected mystery is something I wholeheartedly encourage everyone to embrace.

Shaking things up in your life will lead to more unique interactions and exchanges. If you're always going to the same places, the plot can't twist! It's very hard to add a dash of the unexpected because there is nowhere for it to go! So, make time, room, and space for change and adventure, and you'll suddenly find your days aren't so mundane anymore.

Ideas For Shaking Things Up In Your Day-to-day Life

1. Have the waiter pick something for you. That's right, tell them sweet or savory, and let them decide your fate.

2. Find an entirely new way to get to work. If you typically ride your bike, try walking. Or maybe if you take a bus, try walking and taking the train. If you drive, consider offering to ride-share several days a week.

3. Start going to a monthly meet-up with the goal of meeting three like-minded people you can add to your life. There are meet-ups for everything from soccer to cryptocurrency to wine tasting and scrapbooking.

4. Volunteer. I believe that volunteering is good on so many levels. Not only can you meet a wide range of people from all walks of life, but I believe you are changing your energy positively. Animal shelters. Homeless shelters. Senior care. Services for the disenfranchised. There are so many options, so pick something you care about and want to sink your teeth into. Get passionate about whatever it is!

5. Vacation alone. I understand this is terrifying for most people, and it's an even tougher sell for those with partners. Nonetheless, traveling alone is one of the most incredible ways to connect with like-minded strangers.

6. Attend several high-priced galas and mingle with the room. This one is still on my to-do list, but every year I've hoped to be brave enough to buy $500-$1500 plate

dinner tickets for worthy causes, then work the room like a brazen socialite on a mission. I believe you have to go alone, or you'll never push beyond your comfort zone. I love the narrative I make up in my head about what exciting characters I might connect with, whom I might never otherwise have met.

LET ME TELL YOU A STORY:

One morning, my friend Lulu realized she'd run out of butter. So, she bundled up her newborn baby boy, Blair, and headed to the grocery store. After she'd grabbed everything she needed, Lulu saw a woman, also with a new baby, struggling with a bag of groceries as she was leaving the grocery store. Lulu rushed over and helped her right as the groceries spilled out all over the place. After they'd picked everything up, the two women started chatting, and before long, Lulu invited Sukio—as her name turned out to be—for a quick coffee, and Sukio accepted. The two connected immediately, so their coffee time flew by. Before they parted that day, Sukio invited Lulu to join her weekly mother's group, and Lulu accepted. Little did she know this group would have a massive impact on her life over the years.

In time, Lulu and Sukio became extremely close friends bonding over writing and babies, and eventually, they started a moms writing group. One day, during a 'free write' (a writing exercise where everyone is given a topic and a time limit) the pair discovered that Sukio's husband and Lulu's brother had attended the same summer camp together when they had been in their teens! Funny coincidence since Lulu's son Blair and Sukio's son had become best friends and had also attended the summer camp in question. Time passed and as Lulu's marriage fell apart, Sukio was there for her, their friendship growing stronger all the time. The two of them were even on the phone as the twin towers in New York City fell in September 2001.

I think this is a powerful story considering the pair met randomly in a grocery store. But the tale gets even more amazing. In 2015, Sukio spat in a test tube and sent away for one of those amazing 'Find Your Relatives' DNA tests. Low and behold, among the multitudes of names listed as relatives she saw Lulu's dad's name.

WHAT ARE THE CHANCES? I love the idea that despite all the odds, true family has a way of finding their way back to each other.

What's the Point?

Living a more exciting life requires that you're ready to do the things that make you nervous, uncomfortable, and scared. You must be ready to jump at any and all offers because even something that sounds lame could turn your life upside down.

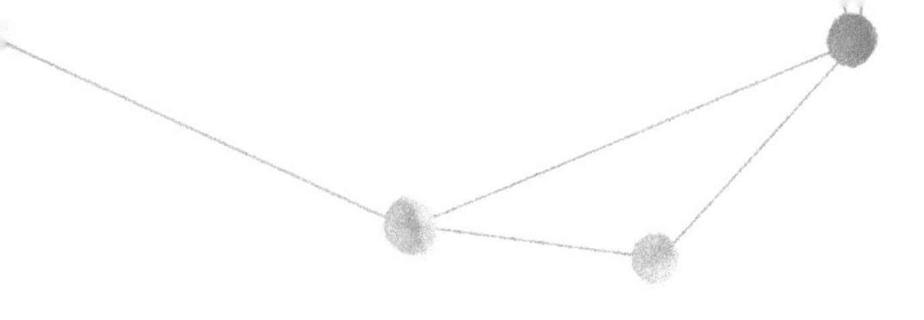

9

Tiny Connections Will ... Turn You into a Super-Connector

What's a super-connector? Allow me to explain. A super-connector is someone who is always cross pollinating their social network. Introducing everyone they know to everyone else. Maybe they do it to help someone get a job, find a better accountant, get married, or maybe they do it because they think the two of them will hit it off. The 'why' isn't important. The important thing is that they do it, and they do it often. It's important because when we are super-connectors, we grow our network, the network of those around us, and our community. Doing that has legit benefits for our health, our hearts, and our mental wellbeing. More than that, being a super-connector can make us invaluable to others.

I recently got a text from Rene that said:

> *Roger and I are trying to find a spa where we could get Valentines massages together—but we've waited too long. Everything is booked up. We both agree, if anyone can help us—it's you!*

I love texts like these, because as a super-connector I enjoy making helpful, game-changing introductions. I keep detailed lists of spas, restaurants, and service providers ranging from massage therapists and private trainers to dermatologists and high-tech endodontists.

My list of connections is extremely valuable, because I am meticulous about keeping it up to date and because I know them all personally … which means they'll call me back. Can you put a value on having a great list of contacts? Absolutely. I was offered a job to run the new business department at a Raleigh ad agency because they knew my ad agency client connections would be so valuable. Many salespeople get multi-million-dollar offers because their list of connections translates into gold for whatever companies they work for. Who you know is everything, which is why I think it's vital to believe that each contact you make is valuable. Sure, some may be more valuable than others—but each and every contact you make has tremendous worth.

Knowing the Right People Makes Life Easier

Another reason it pays to be a super-connector? It saves you time, money, and effort. Having the right people in your phone favorites makes life easier.

Let's say you're craving some spicy soup, but you're not about to make the fifteen-minute schlep in the car to get it unless you're sure it's worth the trip. What do you do? You text your favorite foodie friend to see what she thinks:

Have you tried that new pho place up north yet?

She responds a few minutes later:

It's OK, but not great. You're better off going to the one on the Eastside. Plus they do DoorDash.

Problem solved! You'll get your tasty noodles without having to leave the house. Asking the right person for restaurant advice saves you time, money and maybe a stomach ache. That's valuable.

However, beyond restaurant and vendor recommendations, have you ever thought to ask your foodie friend if one of her friends might be a good friend for you? Would you introduce her to one of your other foodie friends? We never really think twice about asking our friends for advice, restaurant recommendations, or whether they know any cute singles. We'll ask them to set us up on dates or help us get new jobs. So why is it that we steer clear of asking for their help when it comes to making new friends? Some people compartmentalize friends so much that they would never think to introduce work friends to soccer friends, or high school friends to college friends. And some people just don't really think about it, so you have to ask them to make that link.

Connecting your connections (and connecting with their connections) is a fantastic way to meet like-minded humans. You like your friends, they like their friends … if they think you'll get along, it's likely you will. So that's where we'll start.

Introduce New Friends to Current Friends

My whole life I've hosted birthday parties and invited all my friends, from all the different factions of my life. I'd invite my work friends to socialize with the friends I'd made singing at church, going dancing, riding the subway, or volunteering. While everyone may have had different backgrounds, I believed since they are my friends, and they liked me, that there was enough commonality for them to enjoy meeting each other. As a result, I've had friends invest in real estate projects with some of my other friends. I've had friends who have hired my other friends. I once even introduced an acquaintance to a friend, and he married her. I've certainly introduced people who have become each other's closest friends. I take great pride in being able to scatter my friendship seeds and have them grow into something valuable for others.

LET ME TELL YOU A STORY:

Before Facebook, when you were traveling somewhere you knew no one, you would reach out to your network and ask, "Hey, know anyone fun in London?" or wherever it was that you were headed. If you were lucky your friends would give you names and numbers. If you were very lucky, you might even get an invite for dinner or perhaps even an offer to stay on someone's couch.

My friend Robin from London had a business colleague who was coming to New York for some Halloween fun. He asked if he could introduce us, and—adoring Robin as I did—I was open to it. A few days later, I'd heard from his 'good mate,' Sumner, and agreed to meet this British bon-vivant and a bunch of his unruly friends down at a trendy Soho hotel. I was watching my pennies, so I opted to skip the fancy hotel dinner and just meet them for dessert and drinks around nine. When I arrived, this wasn't the intimate affair I had imagined, instead these friends-of-friends had managed to wrangle a group of about ten people who were all having a very lively time.

Everyone seemed to be in a fantastic mood, as it seems my hosts were very entertaining Irishmen who were quite used to drinking large quantities of wine. Dessert done, we stayed for another few hours, opening bottle after bottle, and the next thing I remember I was dancing on a stage in some nightclub.

The whole memory is kind of blurry, but for most of the evening, instead of getting to know Sumner—I'd been chatting with a bubbly, brunette named Alex. She and I were having a whale of a time! Although she was American, it turns out that Alex had met Sumner and his bestie Josh, the night's self-appointed ring leaders, while she was studying at University in Dublin, Ireland. Despite the fact that Alex had fallen madly in love with Ireland, after graduation, she'd come back to New York and was working at New York Magazine—one of my favorite publications. After this classic New York night out, Alex and I went on to be fantastic friends. She invited me to her wedding and has shown up at every single birthday event I've ever invited her to. Over the past twenty-five years, I've introduced her to all my friends, and slowly our friend groups have commingled more and more.

After she left New York Magazine, Alex worked a few different jobs but for the past twenty years, she's been employed by several good friends of mine. Every time she's been at a career crossroads, she's been snapped up by another one of my friends almost immediately upon introduction. I think it's safe to say that neither my life nor Alex's would be the same had I chosen to sit home that night.

That said, Alex didn't end up working for my friends randomly. It happened because I know her well, and I know what kind of work she enjoys doing well. Simultaneously, I know what kind of people my other friends need to work with. Knowing what they each need, and wanting to help them both makes it easy for me to make stellar introductions. This doesn't 'just happen.' Because I am a super-connector, I'm always looking for ways different people can be woven into each other's lives, so that everyone's life is enriched in all sorts of ways.

Any super-connector will tell you that introductions are only the first step. You have to tend to your network if you truly want it to grow. My friend Vincent seems to know someone in almost every city around the world because he grew up a diplomat's kid, traveling the world. After he moved to New

York City in his twenties, he continued to travel extensively and is always meeting new people. Over the years, I've introduced Vincent to several of my friends around the world and I'm amazed when a decade later, I see that they're still friends. I got curious and asked him how he managed to grow his friend base so effectively. Here are his secrets:

1. Reach out regularly over whatever medium is comfortable. Maybe it's email, Wire, Signal, WhatsApp, Instagram, Facebook, LinkedIn, or text.

2. Be responsive to messages or calls. Vincent was quick to point out that people's feelings tend to get hurt when you don't get back to them in a timely manner.

3. Invite people into your life in hopes they'll invite you into theirs. (Vincent used to make a point of asking everyone at Thanksgiving if they had plans and if they didn't, he would include them in his family's festivities. As a Canadian living in New York, I was lucky enough to be included in his family's celebrations on more than one occasion.)

4. Ask your friends to introduce their other friends to you. When you get to know new friends through mutual friends, they will have a higher likelihood of going out on a limb for you than they would for strangers. Maybe that means they'll show you around a new city, country, or they'll take the time to do you a favor.

While it may seem odd to ask friends for introductions in your current city, most of us wouldn't think twice about asking our friends if they knew anyone in a different city. "Who do you know in ______?" could be a life-transforming question depending on the outcome. While the blank space can apply to a geographic destination, it works equally well for an industry, company, or non-profit organization. Never ask for just one introduction, always ask for three, because why stop at one, especially if your friend is well connected?

Introduce them to your friends, and support as much inter-friend mingling as possible. Paying it forward is always a good thing. Unsure about how to kick start a conversation with someone you just got introduced to? Why not try a text on your preferred platform (such as Messenger or Facebook) that goes something like this:

Hi! My name is Jen, and our friend Gerry suggested we'd enjoy connecting when I asked him who he knew who liked going to concerts. I'm in need of more music in my life, and people to enjoy it with, so I was hoping we could grab a coffee / walk in the park / kids playdate …

Finding time for new people in our lives gets increasingly challenging as we age, but many people realize how valuable it is to grow their circles. So be hopeful and don't get discouraged if the first person you connect with isn't overly receptive. That's just one person. Keep trying!

Invite Friends & Acquaintances into Your Home

When we invite people into our home, it can deepen our connection, friendship, and help us bond. Sharing our homes is a deeply personal thing for many of us. Your home is a private and sacred space, so inviting people in can be a vulnerable experience. I know it is for me. But nonetheless, I try to make my home available to my inner circle. This kind of sharing leads to intimate moments over coffee in the morning, or while you're brushing your teeth in the hall and laughing about something. Those connective moments can help you better understand your guests, and they in turn will get a better sense of who you are, which is fundamental for being a super-connector. You've got to know each other well enough to feel comfortable introducing them to friends and colleagues, depending on the situation at hand.

Plus, when friends stay with you, and their friends visit them, your circle grows as well because you're meeting new people on your turf. Opening your home is a great way to deepen friendships, cement ties, and expand your network.

LET ME TELL YOU A STORY:

I once couch surfed (www.couchsurfing.com) my way around Sicily with a partner. Stranger after stranger offered us not just a couch to crash on, but entire homes. They expected nothing in return except the opportunity to hang out, have a meal, and practice their English. It was fun because we got locals to act as tour guides wherever we went and were exposed to experiences we couldn't have stumbled on as outsiders even if we'd wanted to. In Marsala, Sicily—we were ushered onto the top floor of a ferry boat headed to Favignana and Isola di Levanzo, as our couch surfing host, Rubio, was friends with everyone, including the captain of that boat. We spent the next few hours chatting with the boat crew while eating amazing biscotti and drinking delicious Italian liquor.

We would never have been able to do any of that without having an insider show us around. Someone who was part of the local scene and who was willing to open his home and his heart to us. Despite immense language barriers, we stayed friends for a decade through Facebook, and eventually I was able to welcome Rubio and his family in New York City. I was extremely excited and proud to show him around and take him to a few hidden New York gems. While it might seem inconsequential, knowing I have such a grounded connection in Sicily really changes my perspective on traveling to that region of Italy. I feel more confident and automatically connected. That's the power of welcoming strangers into your home.

Help Your Social Network—Network for Work

As a super-connector, I'm never surprised when friends and former co-workers reach out asking for help finding work, even if it's many years since we've spoken. They know I'm a well-connected individual who hustles to stay connected to people I enjoyed working with. When they reach out, I always do my best to assist their search because I hope if I needed work, my community would help me.

While I know that everyone is busy with family, friends, and all the other obligations we typically have, if someone is unemployed and nervous about paying their bills, I am supremely empathetic. This is why I will send emails out to anyone who might be in the market to hire a desperate friend. If I can't make ten to twenty minutes to help someone I care about, by quickly connecting my closest network, what kind of a friend am I?

In return, I hope that those friends who get interviews and work as a result of my efforts will be receptive to me when I reach out in need. This kind of 'you scratch my back, and I'll scratch yours' is not new, but while I hate to admit it, I think people take it for granted. Too often they accept the support and don't give it another thought. I once got someone a job that paid over $90,000 a year, and he invited me out for what I thought was a thank you drink and dinner. Turns out I was wrong. He just invited me out to have drinks. He didn't offer to buy a drink, let alone pay for dinner. I was actually shocked, but I paid my half and lost his number. I am not interested in fostering friendships with ungrateful people. Life is too short.

So, the next time someone reaches out asking if you've heard of any available positions, don't just say you haven't. Ask them to send you their resume, and take a moment to review it. Is there anything you think that needs to be fixed? Does it work for your industry vertical? If it looks solid, why not forward it to any of your friends in HR, or whoever might be hiring. No one is going to hate you because you reached out on behalf of a friend or former colleague. On the contrary, they'll see your super-connector side and admire you for it. When you reach out on their behalf, and let them know what you've done for them, you'll be building more trust and underscoring the importance of effort and elbow grease. Next time you're in need, you'll likely be impressed how others show up for you!

Skyrocket Your Network: Altruistic Networking

If you really want to next-level your connector capabilities, it's important to boost your personal and professional network so you make more money or achieve whatever goals you're setting for yourself. I've developed something I call 'altruistic networking' and it's a smart, fun way to mingle with purpose—I hope you'll want to try it out.

Picture this. You're walking around a gathering, a conference, an office party, or a large meeting with a specific connection goal in mind. Maybe you're trying to meet three new people just to grow your roster of interesting humans? Maybe you're looking for social media influencer types? Or maybe you're trying to get a lead on a specific type of web developer? Whatever it is that you are looking for, as you talk to people ask them if they will keep an eye out for that type of person as they mingle with everyone. Then ask them who they are looking to meet.

For instance, maybe you meet a bubbly gal named Tomoko at a party. Tomoko tells you she's looking for a hot, single guy over thirty-five—because she's single and ready to mingle. What harm does it do for you to ask every guy you chat with who fits the bill if he's single? If he is single, you can call Tomoko over and introduce them under the pretext they have so much in common. Meanwhile, you've told Tomoko you're looking to meet anyone who invests in real estate and you've asked her to introduce you when she connects with them. As the two of you move around the event, don't be surprised if you end up meeting exactly who you wanted to meet—because instead of just you asking around, you now have one or more people keeping an eye out for whatever it is you're looking for. You're scratching their back, and they're scratching yours in perfect altruistic harmony.

Not sure of how to get five to ten people connecting throughout the room on your behalf? Here's the breakdown on how to do it:

1. Spend ten minutes connecting with every person you meet, talking to them about their life, what they're drinking, how their day went.

2. Next, say the following, "I'm here to meet anyone in the (pet care world) because I'm trying to achieve my goal of (opening a vet clinic), and I'd love your help tonight. If you meet any (vets or vet techs), can you please come find me? In return, I'd really love to help you connect with the people you're looking to connect with. Tell me more about who you're trying to meet here."[32]

3. Most people are so stunned by the offer, you'll visibly watch their face soften into amazement. Then typically they quickly agree to giving it a shot.

4. Take out their business card—write down who they want to meet and what they want to achieve, then be sure to give them one of your cards ... hopefully they'll take notes on it as well.

5. Ask them if their cell phone is on, because if you can't find them, you can give them a quick call so they can come find you and meet whomever they need to meet.

6. Now that you've exchanged cards, get mingling. Have this exact same interaction five to ten more times. Exhausting? A little. But at the end of the evening, I promise you'll have a number of people coming over to you, introducing you to others, and hopefully you'll be able to introduce some of your new friends to connections that will advance their goals.

Super-Connectors are 'Top of Mind'

One thing I've learned from lecturing and coaching people and companies on the power of connections is that most of us really don't realize just how important our network is until we've been working for one or more decades. People assume that because I'm a strong, outspoken personality that I've always been aware of the power of connections. Not so. If I had been, I would probably have more than five friends from college days. But eventually, I woke up to the power of my friendships in both my personal and professional life and realized how valuable those pathways were, not just for paying the bills, but for helping me negotiate the earth with grace, kindness, and a sense of belonging. There is true beauty to feeling valued, accepted, and appreciated by your community. There is also a certain amount of social power, because when you make an effort to check in and connect, people think of you for parties, jobs, and all sorts of other opportunities. Being top of mind feels great!

What's the Point?

Want more out of your life? Keep helping others. It's the key. Other people are the fastest conduits to your desired outcomes.

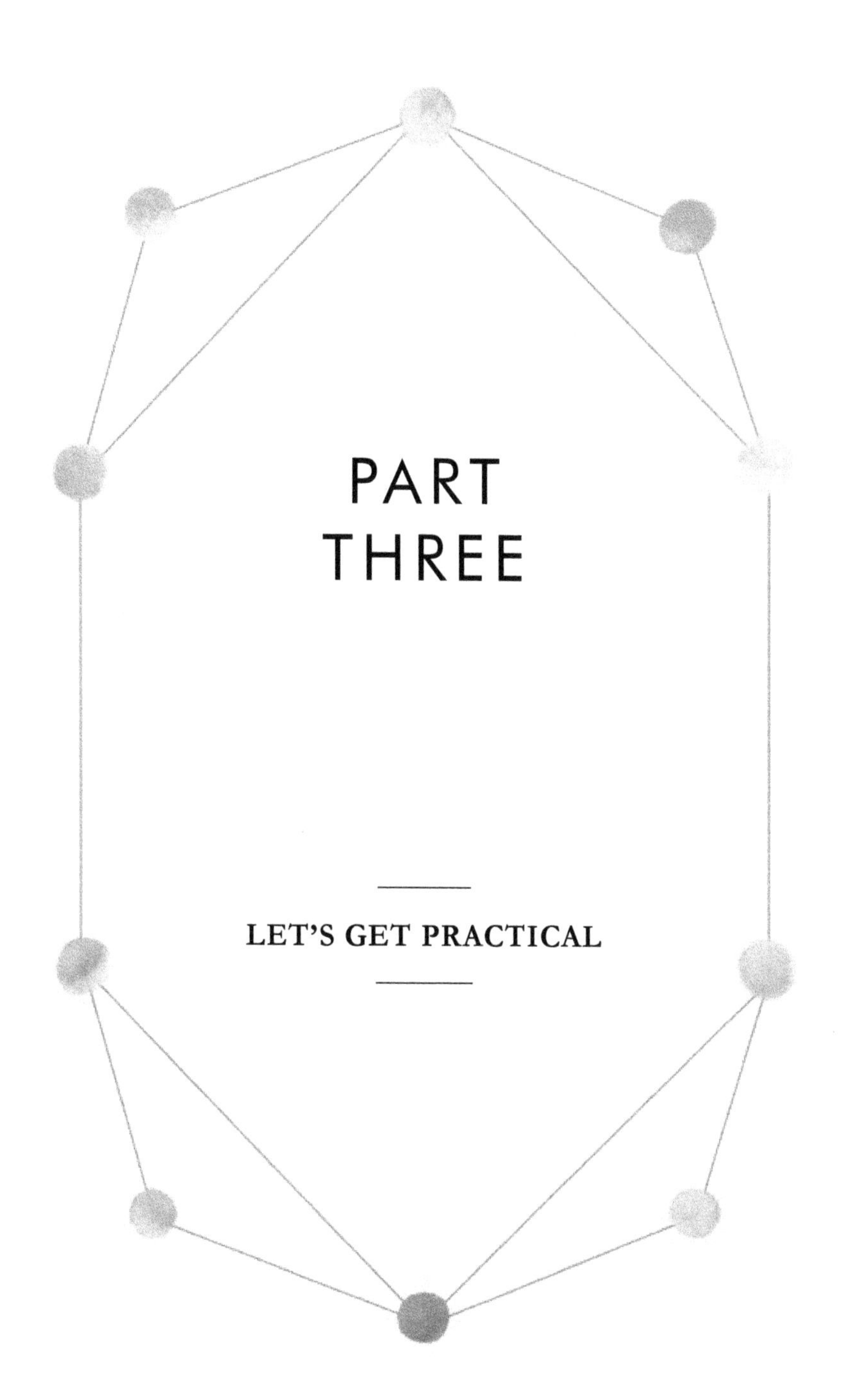

PART THREE

LET'S GET PRACTICAL

Let's Get Practical

By now, you're chomping at the bit to live your most connective and exciting life. While you've gotten the scoop on becoming the life of the party, sparking romance, and making more money or more connections—there are a range of other practical skills you'll find handy at your disposal. Where to meet people and what to wear to make connecting easier. What to say and how to be a better listener. Not in the mood to leave the house? No problem! There are also ways you can connect remotely that can build real rapport. Working from home? We'll also dig into how to create a connected remote workplace. The kind where everyone feels included and appreciated remotely. With this arsenal of approaches, there will be no shrinking your life. It's going to be expanding all the time.

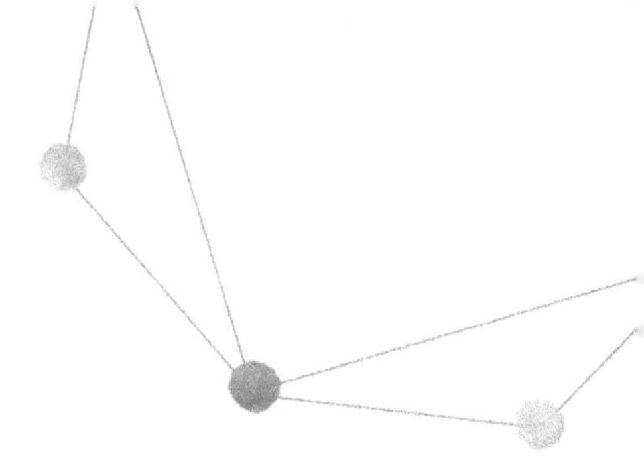

10
Tiny Connections 101

Picture this. You're sitting on your weekly bus commute home. It's Friday, and the 3 p.m. bus is always packed with commuters heading out of the city. The bus ride can be anywhere from three to five hours long, depending on traffic—so you sit down and settle in for the long haul. As you squeeze into one of the last seats available, you have a choice. You can sit and play on your phone, read a book, or you can be bold and engage with the person next to you.

Most people assume the person next to them doesn't want to be annoyed with chitchat. But that's not always the case. On one particular bus ride, I ended up chatting with the guy next to me for most of the ride home. Steve ran a production company in Pennsylvania and had just been hired to do all the puppeteering for the Metropolitan Opera's production of Madame Butterfly. I really enjoy the opera, so I was pretty jazzed to hear all about this, and by the end of the ride, I had scored an invitation to go backstage after a performance. I had a fellow opera lover visiting me the week of the performances, so I booked two tickets immediately. Not only did I get to see an amazing staging of this Puccini classic, but I got to go backstage at the Met and share it with a friend.

While breaking the ice may be as easy as saying, "Hi, I'm Jen," it doesn't always feel so simple. The same way people get tongue tied and freeze before they engage a stranger off the cuff, people also aren't sure how to make a connection.

How to Make a Connection Anywhere

There are so many great places to meet people beyond bars and gyms. People often forget about talking to others when feeling bored. Awesome people await you in lines—to bathrooms, in grocery stores, and queuing for airplanes. Human gems are waiting to meet you on trains, buses, and at little league practice.

Here are some scenarios to jump start your imagination and your engagement. This is by no means an exhaustive list; instead look at it as a list to get you thinking about your life, and where you have opportunities to connect with other people.

Concerts, sporting events, shows: Kick any event off by immediately introducing yourself to anyone sitting around you. In front, behind, to the left and right. I typically say something along the lines of, "Hi, since we're going to be enjoying X side-by-side, can't hurt to introduce ourselves, right? I'm Jen. I've been a fan of X for years …" And if at any point you're going to the bar, offer to get them something from there.

Think about the last time a random stranger paid for something for you—and how amazing it felt.

While it can be prohibitively expensive to buy a beer or two at a concert, if you took this action, most likely later in the evening the recipients of your largesse will return the favor. Even if they don't, buying people you don't know a pretzel or coke could potentially be the highlight of their night. How cool is that?

Look for opportunities to create some space for a late comer, maybe someone who is trying to find lawn space for an outdoor concert. Or save a spot in line for a stranger who needs to run to the bathroom. That type of kindness goes a long way to encouraging dialogue later.

Kids sporting events: You might have to spend a lot of time hanging out at your kid's sports practices during the week, or maybe on Saturday mornings. Maybe you do it all the time, and you know a few people, or maybe you know no one. Try showing up one Saturday morning with a pitcher of virgin mimosas and a pitcher of real mimosas. Bring cups and offer drinks around as you introduce yourself. When you're done, hopefully you gauged who among the other parents and spectators seemed like someone you would most likely connect with—so you can pour yourself a drink and go get connecting! This works with cookies, orange slices, or any other shared food.

Lines of any kind (ticketing, food concession, bathroom, etc.): While I've never made a friend in a bathroom line, it's on my bucket list of things to achieve. However, I did meet one of my oldest friends in a line for housing insurance back in college, while doing a semester abroad. When you think about it, anyone standing in a line is a captive audience which means it's potentially a great time to tell a joke, or ask silly random questions like:

- "How about those Yankees?"

- "How's your day/afternoon/evening going?"
- "I'm working on meeting new people in new and unusual ways. Feel like talking to me?"

Fancy events (ballet, opera, polo): It can feel daunting to connect with people at these types of formal events. People tend to be there in couples or tight cliques, and connecting with anyone requires a certain amount of personal determination. Focus on anyone that catches your eye in the refreshment lines, and strike up a chat about whatever you're seeing. Who knows where it could lead?

Networking events and conferences: The great thing about these types of events is everyone is there to meet new people. Some are selling things you won't ever need, but that doesn't mean you shouldn't connect. Who knows who they know? Typically the best way forward is bold connecting as much as you can handle. Because the tendency is to quickly feel overwhelmed at the prospect of meeting tons of new people, set goals (meet ten new people before you go for lunch) you can psychologically manage, and balance that feeling of being overwhelmed.

It's important to remember you're not just meeting the person you're talking to when you're making a new connection. You're potentially meeting and connecting with every person they know. For instance, if you're looking for a South American distributor for your handmade soaps, while the gift card vendor may not seem helpful at first blush, you have no idea who they might have on speed dial. Everyone you meet could be the perfect link or connector to where you want to go, so you have to give them a shot!

Connect with building operations staff: If you work in a building with a security guard, or any kind of janitorial staff—

why not engage them in conversation? Try something like, "Hi, I've seen you around here for a while. I thought I would introduce myself. I'm ... Where are you from?"

From this day forward, at the very least you'll be able to pass them in the hall and wish them a nice day by name. For all you know, your kids go to the same summer camp, and maybe one day when you have a flat tire, you'll be able to call them and ask them to pick your kids up for you. It's a long shot, but overlaps like this are more common than you'd think.

Quick Tip: I am not great with names, so when someone tells me their name for the first time, I picture the first letter on their forehead and then use their name immediately at least two times. A conversation might go:

> **Me:** Hi, I'm Jen.
> **Amir:** Hi, I'm Amir.
> (I picture a big A on his forehead for the rest of our chat)
> **Me:** "Awesome Amir. So nice to meet you. How long have you been working here?
> **Amir:** Just two years.
> **Me:** That's great. I don't know that many people yet, but hey, now I can say I know Amir!

Transportation seat mates: Buses, trains, subways, planes, uber share rides ... these are all different ways to meet people.

How to Break the Ice

While I've touched on this in different parts of the book, it had to have its own section, because once you do this you're off and running. I suggest you choose obvious, logical ice-breakers rather than the super cheesy lines that can sometimes make people cringe. (Mind you, those lines can still work if delivered in the appropriately cheesy manner!) Pretend you're in some kind of group setting, rubbing elbows with lots of strangers. Do a gut check and see what you're feeling in that very moment. Whatever comes up for you—lead with it. It may be incredibly vulnerable and endearing, which will facilitate connection on many levels.

Here are a few ideas to help you:

- "Hi, my name is … and I don't know anyone here."
- "Oh, look! My favorite—(insert food item that's in front of you)! Do you love these too?"
- "You guys look fun. Can I join your group? I came solo to this shindig."
- "I struggle going to conferences/bars/weddings etc. because they can give me a little anxiety. You don't look anxious at all, what's your secret?"
- "Will you save me from standing by the appetizers? I'm in need of distraction!"
- "Hey, I suck at small talk, but you look bored, so I thought I'd come over and discuss life's greatest mysteries with you." (Have one lined up that you're willing to chat about.)
- "Hi. This is a little random, but I am looking for an (executive coach, mentor, new job in advertising, real estate lawyer, etc.) and was curious who you might know in that space?" (This is a great time to manifest your dreams. Ask directly for what you want.)
- "What's a nice guy/girl like you doing in a place like this?" (Sometimes clichés make the best openers, because people want to laugh. This works especially well when it's utterly random and clearly NOT a pick-up line.)

Another great option is to make it easy for others to break the ice with you.

How to Be a Walking Conversation Starter

It never hurts to make it easy for someone to strike up conversation with you. I always encourage a little eccentricity because it's charming, fun, and quickly noticed. For instance, if you knew you were going to be standing in line for a while (maybe at the bank or in line at Starbucks), imagine what kind of chitchat you might end up having with people around you if you were juggling oranges.

Next time you're listening to a song you love on your headphones while you're in the supermarket checkout line and you're dying to sing along … why not sing along? Who knows, someone might start singing with you. A friend recently had this very thing happen. A catchy acoustic version of 'The Girl from Ipanema' came on in the grocery store, and she started to sing along. She was browsing the produce, and at the chorus, she picked up two avocados and shook them to the beat in the direction of the women to her right. The woman smiled and started singing along to the song and even picked up a pack of carrots, which she waved back at my friend. No words were exchanged, but the two had a moment that left a smile on my friend Jane's face. Could they have gone for coffee and ended up life-long-friends? Maybe. But sometimes a shared moment of silliness is just as valuable.

Whenever you feel like doing something a little different, a little spunky, or a little over the top, I say you do it. The world NEEDS every infusion it can get of your unique personality. Plus, your unique brand of sunshine inspires and encourages people all around you to let their own freak flags fly and have fun doing it.

If You Dress (Boldly)—They Will Notice

When I speak to companies, colleges, and other organizations on the power of networking, one of the points I always stress is dress. What you wear to events can help or hinder you in the connections department. The way you dress can enable people to introduce you to people you'd like to meet or make it harder for them.

When I am talking about dressing, I am typically looking around the room at a sea of gray, black, and navy. Those are the colors most of us resort to because they are safe, they coordinate easily, and let's face it—they don't show the dirt! But when everyone is monochromatic, it makes it much harder to pick anyone out of a crowd. How is anyone supposed to track you down at a conference to introduce you to that developer you were just asking about? How will someone find you at a meet-up? Making it hard for people to help you meet the people you want to meet is counterproductive, so I encourage you to dress with purpose when you're making an effort to connect with others.

1. Don't be afraid to stand out, whatever that means to you. If you want to throw on that old banana Halloween costume before you hit one of the world's largest conference centers, like the Jacob Javits Center—then do it. It will be a great ice breaker and you can tell everyone you meet you wanted to make it easy to connect with them again and again throughout your conference.

2. Wear bold colors, like a hot pink blazer, a bright yellow shirt, or a loud tie.

3. Don't be afraid to accessorize! Toss on a hat, wear a colorful scarf, a wooden bow tie, or maybe a bright pocket

square. NOTE: Hats are fantastic for big event visibility, and when I go to late-night parties, I often put LEDs in my hats for added visibility. Why would I want to make it hard for my friends and potential new friends to find me?

4. Embrace a bold sense of style. Maybe you love Japanese culture, so you wear a broad obi over palazzo pants. Or maybe you adore unusual, patterned suits, so you arrive wearing floral jacquard.

Standing out makes it easy to find you and makes you easy to talk to. Even if the interaction starts with someone questioning your sense of style, it got them talking!

Read a Popular Book

When I was twenty-six, I was reading *Skinny Legs and All* by Tim Robbins on a New York City subway and a tall, handsome guy tapped my book and commented, "Great book!" We ended up chatting until I had to get off the train, but not before we'd exchanged information. While this didn't turn into a forever romance, we did date for a little while, and he's still in my life to this day. I consider him a dear friend, and we love the story of how we met.

Practice Altruism

Pack individually wrapped chocolates, nuts, or snacks, and offer them around on your plane or shared Uber ride. I don't recommend this approach on buses, trains, or subways. Sharing food requires a more intimate setting.

LET ME TELL YOU A STORY:

Over a decade ago on a flight out of San Antonio, I was heading for a layover in Chicago on my way to Philadelphia. Because I tend to forget to check-in for flights on time, I found myself the lucky winner of a seat in the very last row of the plane. Yippee! As I prefer getting on the plane at the tail end of boarding (so I'm on the plane for the least amount of time possible), I wasn't surprised to see there was already a gentleman sitting in the window seat of my row. I silently prayed that no one would sit in the empty seat between us, so we could both stretch out a little over the next few hours.

Minutes later, the flight attendants closed the cabin doors and prepared for take-off. The seat map gods had granted my wish: no middle seat mate. I settled in, got comfortable, and almost immediately realized I was hungry. Fortunately, I had brought along an orange, which I pulled out of my backpack and peeled. I was about to scarf it down, but I felt a little uncomfortable about eating it in front of my seatmate. I was taught from a young age that it wasn't polite to eat in front of others if you weren't going to share your food. I decided to offer Mr. Window Seat half my orange.[33] *He accepted my orange graciously and seemed very appreciative of the gesture. My rowmate was around fifty years old, with salt and pepper hair and a mustache, and he had a friendly face.*

After eating his portion of the orange, he introduced himself as Rod and asked, "What made you offer me some of your orange? I used to be a missionary in Africa where this type of food sharing is totally normal. But it's not common here in the States."

I explained that I was just old-fashioned and had been raised to feel uncomfortable when eating in front of others who had nothing to eat. He laughed appreciatively at this thought. Then I went on to ask him, "Africa? Wow! That's very interesting. I'd love to hear more about that."

Next thing you knew, Rod and I are chatting all the way to Chicago where I found out he was also transferring to a flight bound for Philadelphia. Turns out we both lived northwest of Philly, near Reading, Pennsylvania. What were the odds of two people on a flight out of San Antonio living so close to each other on the East Coast?

As we talked, small life similarities appeared despite our twenty-year age difference. Rod's parents had been missionaries in Japan, so that is where he had grown up, while I'd lived in Japan for five years from the ages of ten to fifteen. Rod met his wife Mary during his first year of college and the two got married after graduation. Mary, a nurse when they met, held deeply spiritual beliefs that aligned well with Rod's, and she was supportive of his spending a year in the seminary after they'd tied the knot. Next, the pair spent time working and studying in Europe before moving to what was then Zaire, now the Democratic Republic of the Congo. Mary and Rod lived and worked in Africa for a total of eighteen years before returning to settle in Pennsylvania in 1998. I'd moved to Pennsylvania in 2004 and was deeply moved by how lovely the picturesque state was.

Our conversation meandered all over the place until we found ourselves talking about bird watching, which was one of his many passions. Rod invited me to join him in witnessing the migration of 150,000 snow geese, which was apparently quite a sight. What an interesting and random invitation! I accepted on the spot. A few weeks later. At 5:30 a.m. on a freezing cold March morning, I drove out to meet Rod. We drank hot chocolate and watched a massive flock of birds swirling into the air. We even caught a glimpse of a bald eagle.

While we had several dinners with our respective partners, Rod and I didn't stay in touch, but I remember the joy I had chatting with him on that plane ride with tremendous fondness. While writing this book, I reached back out to him, and although it had been eleven years since we last spoke, he immediately responded, "Of course, I remember you. That airplane chat with you was one of my favorites as well." Maybe we weren't meant to change either other's lives, or maybe in some subtle way we did. I haven't fully committed to weekends spent birdwatching, but I'm getting there.

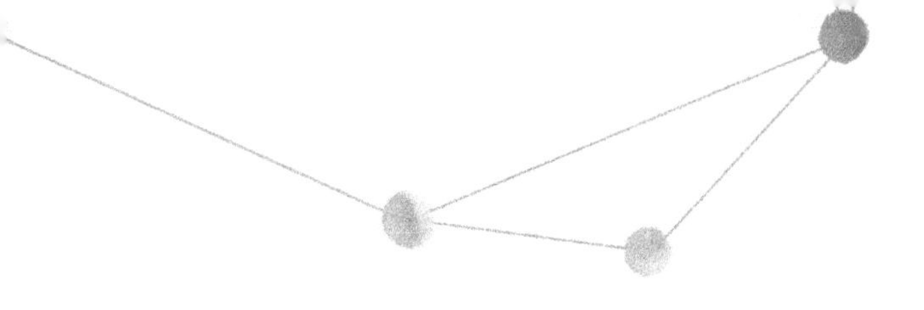

11

How to Work The Room When You Don't Know A Soul

Every person you know has the power to change your life, the same way you can change theirs. So how do you start a conversation with a stranger? The answer is a simple one. Stay in the moment, and go with your gut. If you're in a room filled with strangers and you don't know a soul, open with:

"Hi, my name is … I don't know anyone here."

Nine times out of ten, they'll introduce themselves. You can quickly dive right into connective conversation.

Maybe you are at a conference and your friend just went to the bar for drinks? Run with something like:

"Hi, my name is …. My friend just abandoned me here for the company of the bar. How is your night going?"

I am a massive fan of stating the obvious. It's not so clever as to put anyone off, and it's soothing because everyone knows where they stand. If you're next to a colossal cheese plate, looking for the gouda … turn to the person next to you and just ask,"What do you think, is any of this Gouda? I really love the stuff!"

You'd be surprised at how quickly a silly question turns into discussing what you do, where you live, what kind of dogs you like, and what the best online tutoring services are for teenagers who are struggling with math. The point is, we all feel awkward and uncomfortable when we don't know anyone.

Most of us feel that way when walking into uncertain situations—and most of us are pretty good at hiding it. That's why some of my favorite ways of introducing myself are truly vulnerable. That vulnerability is infectious and engaging and can really resonate with people:

- "Hi … I don't know anyone here …"
- "Hi … my friend just abandoned me to go to the bathroom …"
- "Hi … I came alone, can I hang with your group until the lecture starts?"
- "Hi, are you here alone too? Care to hang out and chat for a bit?"

Don't let the fact that you don't know anyone dissuade you from working the room. You may even find that rolling solo makes it easier to meet people.

12

How to Be a Great Listener

Extensive research[34] has concluded that we remember only about half of what we hear—no matter how carefully we think we were listening. I explored why we're such crappy listeners and discovered that a long time ago, when school curriculums were being designed, schools decided that if a kid could read then it meant they could listen, too. So, the school system saw no reason to teach listening skills. However, now there is data proving that reading doesn't correlate to listening at all. Educators are now realizing that listening is a skill that can and should be taught. In Nashville, for example, the public-school system offers listening training for kids in elementary grades through high school. Several major universities and colleges in the country are also now offering courses in listening[35] and there are free and small fee classes (under $20) in Active Listening on the online platform Udemy.com.

Delving deeper into our poor listening skills, we find that the primary cause appears to be that our brains are fast. We process speech at a much faster rate than the person speaking can get the words out. The difference between the talking speed and the brain's processing speed gives our nimble minds time to goof off, run mental errands, or think about the toppings we're hoping to have on our sandwich later.

There are plenty of tricks for improving your listening skills. A Harvard Business Review article suggests we have to engage in four different mental activities while having a conversation to really improve retention.

Four activities sounds overwhelming. But these activities all work hand in hand when you are intent on listening, and they direct your thoughts to the message being received. The outcome supports very little time left over for those random mental excursions, so hopefully you're hearing from your accountant that you will save big on taxes this year instead of thinking about those sandwich toppings.

Four Tactics for Improving Your Listening:

1. You (the listener) have to think ahead of the talker. That means you try to anticipate where they are going and what conclusions they will draw.

2. You should weigh the evidence used by the talker to support their points, which means you would silently ask yourself: Is this evidence valid? or Is this evidence complete?

3. You should review and mentally summarize the points that the talker has covered so far. (Mental repetition of the main talking points can go a long way to increasing clarity and retention.)

4. Lastly, throughout the conversation you are trying to 'listen between the lines,' hoping to get a glimmer of any meaning that wasn't necessarily spelled out. To do this, you have to pay attention to any nonverbal clues like the other person's facial expressions, their gestures, their tone of voice. What do these clues add to the message your talker is sharing?

If that all sounds way too involved for a conversation with a stranger, try the following:

- Hang on every word the other person is saying
- Keep your face neutral and pleasant so you appear focused and without judgment
- Look at the speaker, eye contact will help keep you more engaged
- Listen. Really listen. Quiet that voice in your head that often yammers on and on like a monkey, and focus on what the other person is saying. There is no rush to respond, even if you feel that there is ... so listen with your ears, head, and heart - and give them that space
- Ask great questions. Ask for clarification
- Reflect back what the person has just said to you, so you are confident you're on the same page

There is no better way to make someone feel heard than to be an engaged listener and to make them feel like there is no place you'd rather be.

The Great Listener Cheat Sheet

Here's the total play book for becoming a better listener. Follow these tips, and you'll go from being a casual listener to someone people truly feel is actively engaged with what they're saying.

Don't interrupt. It's tempting to be thinking about what you're going to say once the other person is done speaking—but better to retrain yourself to focus on listening. Take more time when you respond. Leave a little silence on the table. This will not only help the other person feel heard, but will also support your persona as a thoughtful and reflective listener.

Mirror what was said. It can be extremely helpful to paraphrase what you just heard back to the other person, so they know you're on the same page. You could say something like, "If I'm hearing you correctly, you're trying to convey …"

Make eye contact. Aim to hold the other person's gaze for about 70% of the time that they are speaking. Interestingly enough, if you're speaking, it's suggested you only need to hold eye contact for 50% of the time.[36]

Use good body language. An easy way to make people feel heard is to lean towards them and nod your head occasionally. Avoid crossing your arms when possible, as this can signal you're shutting them out physically and mentally.

Notice nonverbal cues. Pay attention to the person's tone of voice, how they're holding themselves, their facial expressions, and any other indications of their mindset.

Turn off your brain while listening. Stay in the moment. Don't daydream. You can't be thinking about lunch or an errand you have to run and be attentive to someone else.

Ask great questions. Did they say something you're not sure of? Ask for clarification, and while you're at it, ask open-ended questions to help the other person feel more supported. Skip the yes-or-no questions because they can cut conversations short.

Take long slow breaths, and be patient. Remember we're capable of listening much faster than others speak, so take a moment to breathe, and really pay attention to what's being said.

Take a page from the experts. A great way to see how active listening is done, is to watch TV interviews. You might learn a thing or two or see exactly what not to do.

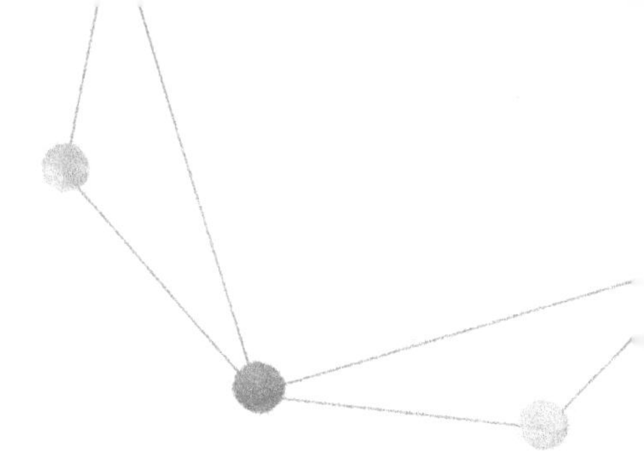

13

What to Do When You Don't 'Click' Right Away

It's human nature to want to feel superior or have more status than others around us. This is a pretty fundamental human trait despite the fact it can be very competitive. In a 2016 research study, participants were willing to lower their social status as long as they were still more esteemed and had a higher perceived social status than others around them.[37] This makes sense when you think about it. Many of us want to be seen as being more powerful or influential than others all around us. But that's not a very helpful trait when it comes to meeting new people and making connections. Getting competitive is a quick way to end any chance of connecting with people because you just made it a win-or-lose proposition, instead of a let's-see-where-this-goes or a what-do-we-each-have-to-offer-each-other proposition.

Someone's status isn't who they are. You can't connect with the physical components of someone's life. Try to connect as humans first. It's okay to be impressed with someone's vintage car if it is a topic you're both passionate about. Asking them questions about how they restored it and learning where they bought it and how they manage to keep it in running order can build a bond between you two. That kind of active and participatory interest is always welcome. Most people are proud of their hobbies and accomplishments and are happy to talk about them at length.

In Chapter Five, we talked about how your body language, tone, and the topics you choose to talk about will all help support a new connection. So, if you're feeling a disconnect, maybe go back and see where you're faltering.

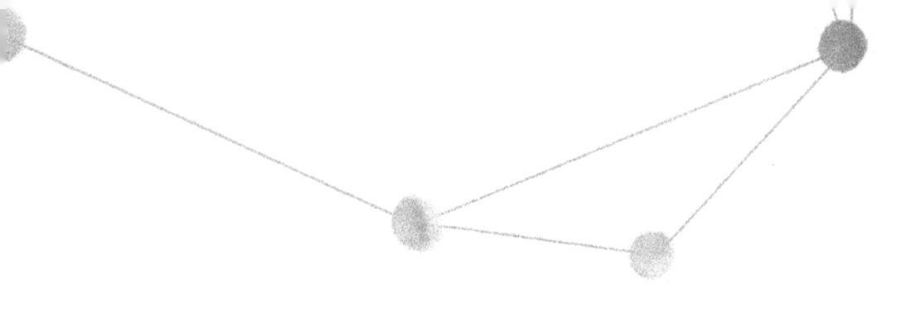

14

How to Exit Conversations Gracefully

I've been asked why I enjoy connecting with strangers, and I think it boils down to a feeling of wild optimism. I'm often wondering random things as I'm meeting new people. I can't help but wonder what if these people will all become my good friends? Where will this night go … if I just go with it? What if we all end up going somewhere cool? What if it turns out we have friends in common?

Staying positive, open-minded, and receptive to new connections is essential, and 99 percent of the time it works out. But on the off-chance it doesn't, here's how to get yourself out of a conversation gone wrong.

Scenario #1: Party

You're at a house party. You've been chatting to a few people for ten minutes and are ready to move on to talk to others. What do you say?

If you genuinely want to stay in touch, take a picture of their card or exchange info, or make a plan and exit right after. Or you say:

"Excuse me for a second, I have to ask Bethany a question."

Or:

"I'm going to grab a drink."

I always try to exit with something positive. For instance, I might pay them a compliment on what they are wearing or reference something they said I found amusing or helpful, so it's a point of agreement restated. This send-off creates a warm feeling.

Scenario #2: Work Function

You're at a work function, and you don't want to be rude, but you need to extricate yourself from the conversation. Slide away with poise by saying:

"I'm sorry, I need to go track someone down, and I know they were leaving shortly."

Then add a compliment that loops back to what you were talking about and reinforces that you appreciated their time and input. You'd say something like:

"I loved what you were telling me about that new software program, and I'll definitely do more reading about that."

Scenario #3: Dinner Party

If you're at a dinner party and the person on the right is very dull, but the person on your left seems to be the life of the party. What do you do? Depending on your mood, you can go a few different ways. If you're feeling mischievous, try to tease the most interesting thing out of your boring seatmate. Get curious and playful with them as you dig into what makes them unique and delightful. They were invited to the party for a reason. See if you can figure out the attraction.

If you're too tired to put in the elbow grease, lean into the fun person's conversation, and every so often ask Mr. or Ms. Boring to chime in:

"Don't you agree?"
Or:
"Isn't that crazy?"

Remember, even the most seemingly boring person might have a lot to offer. They could be hosting the most fantastic party in a month somewhere exotic. They could be casting for a new movie. They could be extremely well connected in a world you're curious about entering. Who knows, they could be your dinner connection jackpot, so keep an open mind, and be as kind as you would hope someone would be to you.

Scenario #4: Transportation Seatmates

If you're on a bus, train, or plane and you really don't want to talk to the person next to you, preferring instead to read your magazine or watch a movie, you can exit the conversation by saying:

"I promised my client I'd have this read by the end of the flight—so I am going to put on my headphones and focus—sorry to be boring."
Or you can say:
"I've had a crazy week, and I'm just going to chill on this flight and try to decompress because it all starts up again when we land! You know how it is ..."

If you chat for a little bit and enjoy meeting your seatmate, you can always take their contact information and apologize for not being more interactive. Hollywood producers, crypto kings, and other people I know have met some of their closest friends on flights.

One big-wig Hollywood producer even reunited with her long-lost (and utterly crushable) camp counselor when they were randomly seated beside each other on a flight back to Los Angeles. They talked the whole flight wondering why they felt so connected before realizing that they'd known each other as teenagers. How crazy is that?

Scenario #5: The-Not-So-Graceful Exit

A brash tech entrepreneur shared that when he is looking for a conversation escape hatch, he likes to burp or fart in an outlandish manner. (He was NOT exaggerating.) His gassy emissions were nothing short of legendary. As you can imagine, the listeners would oftentimes excuse themselves to flee the scene. Having witnessed this tactic personally, it's not for the faint of heart, but it was sometimes amusing and always effective.

15

Staying Connected

Imagine this scenario: You've met someone, and you clicked. You shared a real moment. Maybe you shared a meal? Maybe you exchanged stories and time together at a conference or over a video call? Whatever it was, you are intrigued enough to want to take that moment and grow it so that maybe you'll be toasting each other in twenty years. But how?

People's lives are chock-a-block full of to-do lists revolving around family, friends, work, exercise, travel, and everything else from paying bills to staff meetings. I get it. Trying to shoehorn yourself into someone's life is by no means easy or a given. But it's not impossible.

Staying connected is one part regular reaching out and one-part emotional intelligence. For some, contact and connection are hard-wired into their DNA, while others can be taught how to do it. Because I grew up traveling so much, I learned to reach out to stay connected—more than some. However, that doesn't mean building friendships comes easily to me; it still takes practice and dedication to stay in contact with friends all over.

Here is a step-by-step breakdown of how to grow connections and friendships.

1. Enter people you meet into your contact lists. When you receive new information about them, be diligent about keeping that info fully updated. If you find out their birthday, that's a great thing to add to both your calendar (with an annual repeat) and to your contact notes. Facebook can often be a great source of intel, depending on how their privacy is set.

   Additionally, I have many friends who have children I've only met a few times. As a result, I struggle to remember their names which is embarrassing. Now I include kids' and pets' names in the OTHER INFO section of my contacts.

2. Soon after you meet anyone, invite them to connect on LinkedIn. This keeps you top of mind and cements your recent introduction. Some people have different policies about who they will connect with on LinkedIn, but I'm pretty relaxed about it. Mind you I'm much less open-minded about adding friends to Facebook and would caution you to connect via social media platforms with some care. Why? Because sometimes when people know too much about you before you really get to know each other it's like you've given them the key to your house too soon. It's a lot of personal information so it's wise to be cautious. My rule is if we haven't met for a one-on-one hang, and it's not likely we will in the future—I don't add them on Facebook. Some platforms like Twitter are fine to share with anyone, but many people like having only

people they know well follow them on Instagram. Best to get to know the person a little first before connecting there—unless you asked to follow them on Instagram in person when you met initially.

3. Always start with a 'how can I help this person' mindset rather than a 'what can they do for me' approach. Maybe you discussed a trip they were planning? If so, a great follow-up is a few great restaurants you researched that are supposed to be stand-outs in that city. Or if you were talking about your pets, and you mentioned a fail-proof flea collar. Go ahead and send them the link, making it super easy for them to get it on the spot! This type of energetic generosity doesn't go unnoticed.

4. I love birthdays, which is why I make a point of sending my friends birthday gifts, greeting cards, texts, videos, or I will call them and sing! While many people post public messages on their connection's Facebook walls, a more connective way of doing it is to reach out privately and send them a personal message. This might be the one time of year you're catching up with this person, so that makes it a great time to support whatever filament of connection you have, in a more personal way.

   Holidays are a great way to reach out. I send a lot of physical holiday cards and I have a great way to do this quickly and efficiently. My secret weapon is called Postable and you can find it online at: **postable.com/partner/jennash**

   Pick one of their cards, or upload a photo of your own, write out your message in a pretty handwriting of your choice then Postable will mail it the old-fashioned way. The card arrives stamped, with a hand written address. It's really lovely.

5. When you're wearing something or using a gift that someone gave you, why not send them a note or a photo letting them know you're thinking of them? Maybe you're wearing the sweater your bestie gave you? Maybe you're somewhere that always reminds you of something you did with a former colleague, friend, or family member? Those are great moments to reach out and let them know you're thinking about them. Take a photo of yourself in the sweater, or in that special place and send them a text or email. Or better still, upload that photo to Postable and send them a card in under 5 minutes. They'll have something to stick on the fridge or frame.

6. You can get retro-cool and send friends or family members postcards. Other generations love tactile reminders that you were thinking of them, somewhere special.

7. When people reach out asking for your help, make the time.

8. It's always a good idea to be kind to anyone looking for advice because your kindness has the potential to change their life. They may be older, or younger, it doesn't matter. I find that if possible, being kind is always the best way forward, plus I believe in Karma and want the universe to be kind to me.

9. Be old-fashioned, and just call someone out of the blue. People don't call each other much anymore so we're often shocked when someone we know does reach out. Why not? Talking on the phone is very connective.

10. Did you meet someone through work channels, and you'd like to focus on growing that potential business opportunity? Following up via email is expected, but once

that initial exchange is completed—then what? I think it's fine to reach out every so often, but not more than every six weeks. Perhaps you check-in every quarter, as you never know who might need something, and if you reach out at the right moment, good things might happen when you're top of mind.

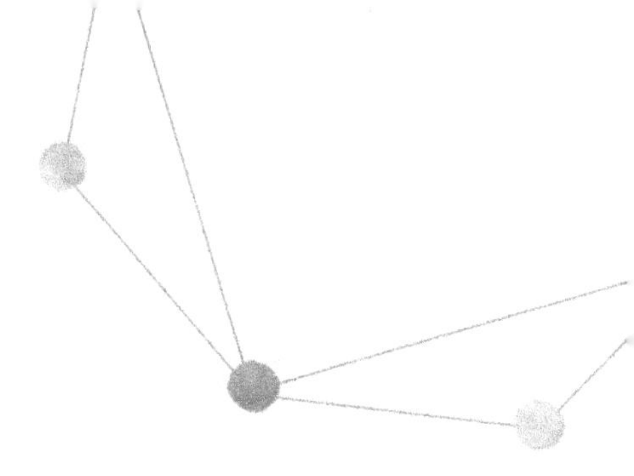

16

How to Connect Without Leaving the House

I've got some excellent news—connections don't only happen in person. They happen almost anywhere we connect heart and soul with other humans. That means these connections are happening in chat rooms, on user-created boards like Reddit, in the comments sections of articles and, of course, all over social media. You can even be more targeted when it comes to online connections, because you can specify what types of people you'd like to connect with, then look to chat with them in logical places. For instance, if you want to connect with people who love to travel, you'd connect using keywords and tags on social feeds or on travel sites, boards, or within Facebook groups.

LinkedIn

While I believe that connecting on LinkedIn works, I think requesting that people add you as a contact isn't always the best way. I rarely check that area of LinkedIn. Instead, comment on articles they've shared. Watch to see what they're commenting on and jump into that conversation. Take an interest in what interests them, and try to build a rapport. You could even try posting articles you think they would find interesting, then reach out and connect. That way when you reach out, you're offering interesting content as well as being a potential new business contact.

Article Commenting

Commenting on any article is a great way to connect with the author, as is sharing their article, and helping them grow their audience in any way. I find it's always best to think about what the other person wants and needs, in order to reach out in someone's good graces. If someone's written a Medium article, I always make sure I've clapped fifty times (that's right, you can clap that many times for anything) and share it to other social media platforms. If I can find their accounts on LinkedIn or Twitter, I try to tag them, so they see that I'm sharing their content. This will potentially make them more receptive when I reach out later with my follow-up questions or thoughts.

Social Media Chatter

Commenting on Instagram, Twitter, or other social media in an effort to connect with people posting or commenting, can lead to meeting people off the platforms. People might recognize you at an event, or maybe you'll recognize them. While most of the time people do this to grow their brand, or have the person with more followers mention them, you can also do this when you're just excited about whatever they're posting. Maybe you love following stories about free divers or rescued puppies. Seeing who comments regularly on the different feeds can lead to different online friendships and connections.

Online Talks & Conferences

Have you attended online talks, conferences, or seminars where they had digital break-out rooms so attendees can discuss specific topics in a more intimate circle? Those break-out rooms are a great time to share ideas, and, if you'd like to follow up offline, they make it easy for you to simply ask the whole group, "Hey, since this is such a short break-out session I'd love to follow up after. Can you please put your email or cell in the chat window?" You can say this and type it into the group chat so everyone can shoot you back their info. Of course, if you only wanted to connect with a select few, most messenger platforms make chatting with specific attendees a cinch. While it might seem forward, awkward, or too pushy to ask anyone for their contact information, you will be surprised by how easily most people are willing to share it with you after having spent a little time with you one-on-one. They see you're not a lunatic, so why wouldn't they want to connect further? You're great!

Take Advantage of Introduction Apps & Platforms

I recently had a lunch date over Zoom with a stranger thanks to Lunch Club (lunchclub.ai), a website a friend shared with me that promised smart introductions to relevant people. When I heard about this site, I immediately loved the concept, so I signed up. I figured that in the middle of a global pandemic, something like this would have a very high likelihood of success. It's a safe, affordable, and easy way to meet people, and it makes life very easy for anyone who isn't sure they like in-person interaction.

There is also https://www.internations.org/ which will introduce expats to each other, as they move all around the world. While you do need to pay to get the platform to unlock, one friend met her current boyfriend on the platform, so it does have the potential to connect you to interesting folks, which I think is absolutely worth paying for.

Did you know the Bumble dating app has a BFF and a BIZZ area in addition to their primary dating app? The BFF area of the app is described as helping you to 'expand your social circle (and) create meaningful friendships' while the BIZZ was created so that 'professionals (could) connect with each other, share, and learn.' Technology platforms understand that we are getting more and more siloed in our social networks, so they're making it easier for us to branch out in a way that's most comfortable. If you can't meet face to face, you still have tons of options, so hit up Google and see what might be available to support growing your friend and colleague network.

While on the subject of dating apps, I often use Tinder or Bumble just to meet people online (or offline). I make it very clear in my profile that I'm looking to meet other awesome humans and have no romantic inclinations. But meeting other people through these apps can facilitate jumping on a call, a Facetime, a Zoom, etc. Maybe when you're ready to leave the house? There will be someone fun to meet.

Good Old-Fashioned Phone Calls … and Text Messages

Look no further than your list of contacts when it comes to getting introduced to others. If you're under the age of thirty-five, the idea of picking up the phone and calling someone without an email or text message exchange is potentially terrifying. People just don't do that! I've even been told that it's not polite to call someone without having pre-arranged it. Hogwash!

People don't have to answer their phones if they don't want to, but you certainly have the right to call them, especially if it's between the hours of nine a.m. and five p.m. on a workday! If someone suggests you connect with one of their contacts, why not just dive right in with a good old-fashioned phone call. The introduction is obvious: "Hi, it's (your name), and (friend's name) suggested we should connect because I (insert your skills, value add, connection points), so I thought I would give you a ring. How is your day going?" Naturally if this is all sounding horribly impossible to you, a text message is also likely to do the trick, but you won't end up drinking margaritas somewhere an hour later, because you do lose the tone, excitement, and random thrill of an unexpected phone connection when you go that route.

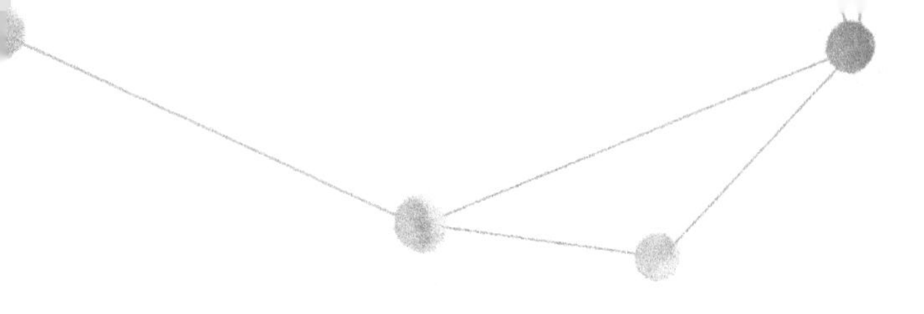

17

How to Create a Connected Workplace

Being properly 'resourced' at work (when your company makes the best use of all your skills) is important when it comes to employees feeling valuable and engaged. Engaged employees are happier because they feel more connected to their coworkers, their work, their office culture, and the company's purpose or mission. Happier employees stay working for companies longer, and retention reduces a lot of corporate spending since it costs upwards of 20 percent of an employee's salary to hire a replacement. Better to keep your employees happy, motivated, and engaged. But how?

Support Employees Becoming Friends

When companies support employees becoming friends at work, they support a happier workplace, which boosts employee satisfaction by 50 percent.[38] Plus, people who work with a close friend are seven times more likely to be fully engaged with their work than if they didn't work with someone they liked.

"We desperately need more leaders who are committed to courageous, wholehearted leadership and who are self-aware enough to lead from their hearts, rather than unevolved leaders who lead from hurt and fear."
— Brené Brown

In my corporate training programs, I underscore this type of thinking and outline ways companies can support their growth goals, while also supporting better co-worker and management relationships. At the end of the day, better communication and connection means people feel more appreciated, are happier, and are more productive which supports the company's growth and profitability. That's the benefit of truly great leadership skills.

Make Daily Connection at Work Easier

Leveraging different chat platforms and meeting technologies like Microsoft Teams, Yammer, Slack, or Zoom is a great way for companies to organize people, projects, files and give everyone a bit of that comfortable watercooler vibe. This helps employees get more involved in the workplace professionally and personally. Slack, for instance, helps groups working on a project communicate more effectively and is great for knowledge sharing. Is there a TED Talk-like presentation starting in the cafeteria? Inviting the whole company becomes a cinch. Hate seeing food go to waste in conference rooms after big meetings? Start a 'Free Food' Slack, like I did at one of the biggest ad agencies in NYC. I could broadcast photos of food and which conference room it was in to the whole company in seconds. We suddenly didn't have a food waste problem anymore. This type of sharing and caring brings people together and gets them interacting. All these platforms are good places to run polls and survey your teams about whatever you're trying to find out. Would they rather get small bonuses or have a holiday party? Would they rather take Presidents' Day or Martin Luther King Jr. Day off? Giving employees a voice can go a long way to making them feel heard and underscoring that their opinions matter—plus it keeps everyone talking and connecting.

Set the Example

From getting everyone to attend the monthly meet and greet, to encouraging all employees to join in for holiday cheer, how leaders promote connection is critical. Leaders set the tone for people in the organization and help everyone understand the importance of creating a connected team. Additionally, they must make an effort to regularly connect with remote employees to reinforce they are a central part of the team. Leaders encouraging participation, communication, interaction, and friendship are supporting a happier, more engaged workplace—all of which ultimately benefits the bottom line.

Schedule Weekly All-Team Meetings

Depending on the size of your company, you will want to look at different ways to schedule meetings. Smaller companies might get the most bang for their buck if they do weekly video calls so that everyone can quickly check-in and outline where their time is being focused. Larger companies might want to have monthly departmental video meetings and weekly team meetings so that everyone knows what they are personally responsible for achieving and can see the bigger picture. While people can lose focus in meetings where they aren't personally engaged, if managers are more strategic, there are ways to keep people focused. One such way is chat polling, which is when moderators post questions into the group chat for the Zoom or Teams meeting, or they ask people to submit opinions. The more engaged and connected people feel, the happier they are in their jobs. Also, you're less likely to be scrolling through your phone during a meeting when the team is constantly asking for your input and feedback.

Host In-Person Meetings and Video Calls

Giving employees different ways to interact with each other gives them many opportunities to connect, assimilate into corporate culture, and get a better sense of each other. Having a mix of both video calls for valuable face time and physical meetings when possible—will help build rapport between the staff members and familiarity with the project work at hand.

Pair Employees for Weekly Remote-Walks

Boost morale, connection, and employee happiness by getting employees to go for walks together. Giving teammates assigned leg-stretching time can strengthen your office culture and offers a host of other benefits.

How do you do this? Try having managers assign walking buddies at the beginning of each month, and making a 20-minute walk together mandatory. Whether the employees are onsite or offsite, they'll get to know one of their colleagues better and get a little fresh air. Mind you, this probably only works in the warmer months of the year. Snow would definitely make this a tough meeting to take.

Create a Private Facebook Group

A private Facebook group can be a great solution for connecting employees. For instance, it can be a great onboarding portal where you upload training videos, share personalized welcome messages from other staff members, or showcase anything that helps create a sense of your company's culture. Additionally, Facebook may be a great place to host live company meetings as it supports real-time interaction.

Use the Chat Box

Your company must get on the chat and meeting bandwagon (think Slack, Microsoft Teams, Yammer, and/or Zoom) so everyone feels as connected as possible throughout the workday.

Pay Attention

The core of connection isn't proximity, it's attention. I typically live on the East or West Coast of North America while many of my best friends live around the globe. Nonetheless, we're still very close and connected. How? Because our attention is on each other. We call, text, Facetime, and are constantly sharing real-time updates which keep us connected. Do the same with remote staff. Pay attention to them, and insist they do the same with you.

Be Inclusive

Reach out informally to remote staff several times a month. Ask them about their families (keep notes on spouses, children, pets so you always seem well informed and thoughtful), their schedules, and what they're binge watching currently. Just ten or fifteen minutes every two weeks will go a long way to having them feel more included and involved.

Don't let Remote Workers Feel 'Out of Sight, Out of Mind'

As the world's workforce evolves and shifts to embrace

both remote and onsite workers, the companies that make thoughtful inroads to supporting their staff are going to be in stronger positions down the road. The flexibility of working offsite might only seem like a challenge to companies used to having 'butts in seats', but with locational flexibility comes the ability to hire the right talent—not just decent talent that's geographically desirable. More and more talented humans are realizing they want to be remote. They gain hours they used to lose to commuting, and as it turns out, can be as productive, if not more, working from home.

The focus then becomes how do we help our remote teams feel connected, when we don't see them as often as we might have years before? From adding their photo to your website in the 'About Us' section, to having a desk with someone's photo on it in your main office, there are lots of great ways to keep an employee feeling engaged, connected, and part of the team. If having a desk isn't logistically feasible, mount photos of your remote employees on a prominent wall in the office. You'd be surprised by how often remote workers are left out of the picture (literally) and forgotten when it comes to supporting your company culture.

Get Virtual Staff Involved in Celebrations

When you hold in-office celebrations, send cupcakes to your remote staff to help them feel included. If your company does a monthly happy hour, why not send them a bottle of something once a month? Make sure your remote staff are not awkwardly watching a room full of co-workers drinking and mingling. Assign several coworkers the task of chatting with the remote workers in a Zoom breakout room for ten minutes consecutively. Make the remote staff feel considered and included.

Plan Team Bonding Events in Each Remote Location

Why not create a scavenger hunt that works in any city and then invite all corporate locations to get busy on a specific date? These types of fun activities encourage inter-office competition and can encourage employees to bond across states, provinces, or even country divisions. It can be as simple as a challenge to other corporate offices or something to help employees from distant branches engage with each other.

Conclusion

LET ME TELL YOU A STORY:

When I was six, I was terribly impressed with Mrs. McClain, an elderly widow who lived down the lane from my family's house in Kingston, Canada. Whenever my younger brother and I wandered by her house on our way to the nearby park, Mrs. McClain would invite us in for tea or lemonade and, of course, cookies. While we were visiting with her, she always told us to help ourselves to one nicely wrapped gift from her 'Present Drawer.'

The Present Drawer was the bottom drawer of a white, ornate chest of drawers that had a privileged spot in Mrs. McClain's living room. She had filled the drawer with individually wrapped gifts reserved for visiting children's curiosity. I don't remember what was in any of the packages I opened, or if I even liked any of them; none of that mattered in hindsight. My entire memory of these moments was the sheer delight of all the unexpected possibilities I could unwrap. I thought Mrs. McClain was the most gracious of hostesses. I loved the simple way she created excitement, drama, and engaged everyone who visited her. It's a gift I have strived to recreate for others my entire adult life.

Let The Surprise Be Your Guide

Those gifts were a bridge into each child's delight. As I grew up, I came to understand how meaningful and wonderfully connective little surprises could be even for adults. Surprises convey to others that you thought about them when they weren't around, that you understood them, and that you made plans, bought something, or took action solely to delight them. As we take in what the other person is doing, sharing, showing, or gifting us with, we get a sense of ourselves, our relationship to that other person, and sometimes to the world at large.

Showing up to a movie theater with a carton of milk, a bag of cookies, and two paper cups can sprinkle a regular outing with magic thoughtfulness. Getting someone's car detailed and leaving them a cute card on the dashboard is a simple, unexpected gesture that can suddenly make someone's day better. Bringing a variety of donuts to work, including some gluten-free and vegan options, shows you're next-level thoughtful and that you understand people's priorities. You didn't have to do any of these things, but you went out of your way to create moments to show those around you that you see them, understand them, and genuinely appreciate them. You're making connections, bonds, and community with every act of kindness, generosity, and care. I live my life looking for these opportunities.

It gives me so much joy to infuse anyone's hum-drum moment with something unexpected. I want those around me to feel cherished and special, because I hope, in turn, our bond will deepen. Creating connection is my purpose and mission and I hope to inspire you to find the sweet spot between doing what you're great at or what you love and how you can connect in with others. For me, connection is it. I believe in connection and its power to reshape our world for the better.

Positive Habits Are as Contagious as Negative Ones

I used to get extremely annoyed with people who didn't pick up after themselves, who spilled popcorn all over a theater and left their mess for the attendants to pick up. I am not a fan of this type of behavior. Attendants shouldn't be cleaning up after a room full of adults who can pick up their own trash. Nonetheless, lots of people have no issue leaving their sodas and snack packages on the movie screening floor, and in doing so, they influence their neighbors to do the same.

Psychologists Victoria Horner and Andrew Whiten ran a famous study[39] in which two test groups—three and four-year-old children and chimpanzees—were shown a box with a treat inside. In one setting, the box was opaque, while in another, it was transparent. The kids and chimps were shown how to open the box to get the treat, but the experimenters also included an irrelevant step: tapping on the box with a stick.

The kids carefully copied all the steps to open the box to get their treat, even when they could see that tapping the stick had no discernible effect. In other words, the kids copied irrationally instead of doing only what was required to get the treat. Sure, the kids were young, but additional research has shown that older kids and adults are even more likely to copy others' actions mindlessly. (Surprisingly, young infants are less likely to copy not-so-logical or impractical behaviors.)

On the other hand, the chimps in the Horner and Whiten study only over-imitated when they couldn't see through the opaque box. When the box was transparent, they saw that the stick was mechanically useless—the chimps ignored that step entirely and just opened the box with their hands. Net-net? When it comes to copying behavior, the apes were more rational than children or adults—but more importantly, humans tend to mimic others' behavior.

Did you know that if someone rubs their face while you're talking, you'll rub your face? Or if they start shaking their foot, you'll likely follow suit? Humans are natural mimics. Moreover, we are more likely to 'like' people who are mirroring us. We unconsciously notice them copying us and unconsciously appreciate it! So, it goes without saying that each of us can create a social responsibility ripple effect every time we're out in public. When others see us picking up our trash, helping older people across the street, or shoveling our neighbors' walkways, we inspire them to do the same.

We have the power to create a chain reaction of altruistic acts because we're more likely to perform feats of generosity after we've just watched someone else be generous. It's this kind of altruism that can make waves through your community, inspiring dozens of individuals to make a difference. When someone's grocery bag breaks open, and you rush to help—you're not only impacting the broken-bag person's day. You're impacting every person who sees your act of kindness. When people witness a stranger's random kindness; they are filled with hope and joy. Looking for opportunities to help others and improve the happiness of the other strangers around you could and should become a national pastime!

When your city-dwelling friends remind you to take a look outside your car BEFORE you open the car door so you don't hit a cyclist, you gain even more awareness of your surroundings. When your partner leaves money in the hotel room right before you're about to check out, and you ask what they are doing, you learn that around the world it is customary to tip the housekeeper approximately $5-10 a night for having taken good care of you during your stay. All of this is a learned behavior that supports a potentially kinder, safer, healthier world where we try to be aware of those around us and their well-being.

When it comes to our human connections, learned social behaviors teach us different styles of connection. When we were children, our parents likely introduced us to all the adults who were attending some family function so that we learned the formalities of proper introductions. When your friend Katy emails to introduce her friends Yoon and Carlos, and you BCC Katy in your response, so she is aware you responded—but is not bothered by future communications—that's proper email etiquette. And when you watch an expert networker shake hands around a room and connect with over twenty people an hour with grace and ease, you witness a cadence for easy, fast, efficient greetings. These types of interpersonal connections are learned from watching others and being taught. They are not inborn.

As we mimic and learn, we are sharing and spreading positive behaviors. We become behavior leaders. Our kindness, generosity, and thoughtfulness become the inspiration for those watching us. Maybe it's your kids? Your neighbors? Friends and family, or the people on your block? Every little thing you do that supports connection, kindness, and positivity is powerful. When we're intentionally kind and connective, we leave room for a whole world of magic to unfold.

You don't know how the person will react when you open the car door for them while they're unloading groceries in a parking lot. They might invite you on their boat, which could turn out to be a tiny fishing boat or maybe a catamaran that sleeps four. How did you manifest that moment in your life? Well, you were kind. You were present. You were empathetic, and you genuinely wanted to help.

When we are nice and connect with people, the world becomes a more connective and, arguably, better place. It's that simple. Holding doors open for people and helping pack groceries into trucks is very simple, and it's that simplicity that makes everything possible. We just have to make a choice to do it, and in return the universe may just swing a big bouquet of energetic 'thank yous' our way. What will that bouquet look like? Who knows? But typically, it's pretty awesome.

What About Kismet?

A lot of people think stuff happens because it's meant to happen. It's fate. It's destiny. It's kismet. In other words, you can't really make things happen a certain way because the universe is more fated than that. That's a tough one. I want there to be room for magic in our lives. I want there to be room for cosmic miracles.

I struggled for a long time to understand what the word kismet meant before I gave in and accepted it was just a synonym for the words fate and destiny. I did find it interesting that the word kismet comes from the Arabic word *kismat*, meaning division, portion, and lot. Your lot, as in your lot in life or your fate in life, has a more active vibe to it. It feels like the right word to use when things align and fall into place, as if by magic.

For instance, have you ever wondered if meeting someone at a certain point in your life was meant to be? Were you meant to be on that train, going to that destination possibly just to meet that person? Or were you seated next to each other so you could share stories about the cancer treatments your family members were going through?

You've probably discussed these ideas at one time or another, and boil the whole thing down to the question: Do you believe in fate? Destiny? Kismet? Do you believe there is a grand scheme to things?

When answering the question about if something is fated, I'm not sure if your beliefs really matter because at the end of the day, if you meet someone who tilts the path of your life, and it's life changing—do you really care if it was meant to be? It happened, and your life changed. YAY! So be it. Planned or unplanned, the outcome shifted things for you and the course of your life.

I would hope that everyone has a story about how they went somewhere and met someone who influenced them for years to come. Maybe a bartender giving travel advice, a kind stranger offering you a palatial home in a foreign country, or maybe a tech entrepreneur who totally changed how you approach life.

LET ME TELL YOU A STORY:

I once got in a disagreement with a total stranger while touring my old high school in Ottawa, Canada. We were walking through the small gymnasium, which had been the library while I was attending the high school. As the tour guide noted we were obviously in the gym, I blurted out to the tour group that the gym used to be the library 'back in the day' —when a very large, tall man who was also on the tour quickly corrected me, insisting that it had always been a gym. I held my ground because for the two years I went to that school—that room had absolutely been the school's only library. Drystan (the larger-than-life gent) disagreed with me and insisted again it was always a gym—so we fell quiet as we both realized neither one was going to change their tune. Ten minutes later, a lively twelve-year-old gave the tour group an overview of the art room. She was so composed and charming, I randomly exclaimed to Drystan, or anyone around me, "Wow. What a kid. Isn't she spunky!"

He responded, "Thank you. That's my eldest!" Ha! I didn't see that coming. We started chatting and I quickly learned that all three of his girls attended that school and that he lived in the Caribbean on the exact island to which I'd just booked a trip. What are the odds that someone on a high school tour in Canada—lived on the very same remote island I was heading to? I was so struck by the coincidence (if that's what it was) that I immediately asked Drystan for his email address so I could follow up for restaurant recommendations.

While our paths didn't cross on the little island in the sun, over the course of the following years, we became friends and eventually started a company together. In time we fell in love, moved in, got engaged and dreamed big dreams together. Over the next few years, we lived between New York and his island in the sun, traveled, and worked around the world in countries like Canada, Grand Cayman, Colombia, Croatia, Bahamas, Greece, the United States, and for several years lived a pretty big life together. We even made it as far as setting a wedding date, getting a marriage license at City Hall and inviting everyone. Pretty nuts considering we met chatting in a library-gym on a high school tour, right? Then came a tiny little thing called the pandemic, and well . . . I think you can guess the rest. While this isn't the fairy tale ending you might have been expecting in a section about Kismet, I can safely say we were both deeply changed by the time we spent together, and neither of us sees the world in quite the same way anymore.

Stay Curious and Hopeful

The notion that there are powerful human connections possible at every turn in your life is very motivating, if those kinds of associations are exciting to you. Nothing can be more inspiring than wondering:

- Where will this go?

- What could this turn into?
- How can I affect their world?
- How can they affect my world?

When you meet someone new, it's not unusual to behave in a way you might not normally consider appropriate. Sometimes that means we're more off the cuff with people that we don't think we'll ever see again. So why not toss out a funny comment to someone waiting near you in a long line? Or crack-up laughing at something a stranger just said to someone else on their cell phone? It's also likely that you might share things of a personal nature more quickly than you would normally. There is an unspoken sense that goes something like, "I'm not going to see you again—so I am going to tell you my dreams!" Dreams come in all shapes and sizes, but when we share them with the world at large, we're making them more real, more tangible, and ultimately, we're increasing the likelihood we can manifest them in reality. Go ahead and share your dreams with strangers. See where it goes.

LET ME TELL YOU A STORY...

Bianca was a twenty-two-year-old American tourist visiting London. She was excited to take in the sights like Big Ben, Westminster Abbey—and of course, all the royal palaces. One day, while waiting in line in a bank to get more British pounds, a man standing behind her in line exclaimed: "Hey! I have those shoes." Looking down, sure enough, they were both wearing identical shoes. Bianca was amused and quickly realized that Josh was a fellow American also visiting London. Josh looked to be about a decade older than Bianca and seemed very kind, but after the two introduced themselves and exchanged pleasantries, they both got their cash and went their separate ways.

A few days later, Bianca was wandering around famous Piccadilly Square and happened to look down and see those familiar shoes again. Sure enough, Josh was sitting there on a park bench. This time they both agreed the meeting was clearly fated, so they went for coffee and a bite. They had a great chat over sandwiches, but after lunch, they again went their separate ways.

Several days later, Bianca was at Heathrow airport as it was time to fly back to New York. However, things weren't looking good, as her flight had just been canceled.

An alternate flight which was leaving later that day had open seats, but they were much more expensive. Shocked at the new airfares she was hearing, Bianca was in the middle of begging the ticketing agent to see what lower-priced options might be available when she heard a familiar voice behind her offering to pay for her seat. Bianca turned around and saw a smiling Josh holding out his credit card.

The two flew back to New York sitting side by side and continued getting to know each other. Despite the fact she offered to pay him back once in New York, he insisted that she not worry about it.

I love this story. It just blows my mind in terms of what can happen when you have two short conversations with a stranger—who is suddenly not so strange after all.

It Is Never Too Late To Connect

LET ME TELL YOU ONE LAST STORY:

In 2006, students at Xavier High School in New York City were given an assignment by their English teacher, Ms. Lockwood. In order to test their written persuasive skills, they were asked to write their favorite author and request that he or she come visit the high school. Several students chose to write to Kurt Vonnegut, the famed author of several highly-respected books including Slaughterhouse-Five and Breakfast of Champions. While Vonnegut didn't end up coming to the school, he wrote the class this wonderful letter:

November 5, 2006

Dear Xavier High School, and Ms. Lockwood (and students)

I thank you for your friendly letters. You sure know how to cheer up a really old geezer (84) in his sunset years. I don't make public appearances anymore because I now resemble nothing so much as an iguana.

What I had to say to you, moreover, would not take long, to wit: Practice any art, music, singing, dancing, acting, drawing, painting, sculpting, poetry, fiction, essays, reportage, no matter how well or badly, not to get money and fame, but to experience becoming, to find out what's inside you, to make your soul grow.

Seriously! I mean starting right now, do art, and do it for the rest of your lives. Draw a funny or nice picture of Ms. Lockwood and give it to her. Dance home after school and sing in the shower and on and on. Make a face in your mashed potatoes. Pretend you're Count Dracula.

God bless you all!
Kurt Vonnegut

Vonnegut nails it, don't you think? Do things 'not to get money and fame, but to experience becoming, to find out what's inside you, to make your soul grow.' This sums up why living life way outside your comfort zone and connecting with others is so deeply valuable. In those bold, connective moments, you'll find art, poetry, dance, humor, and so much joy. You'll also find the biggest, best version of yourself; and allow the people you connect with to do likewise. That is the truest gift.

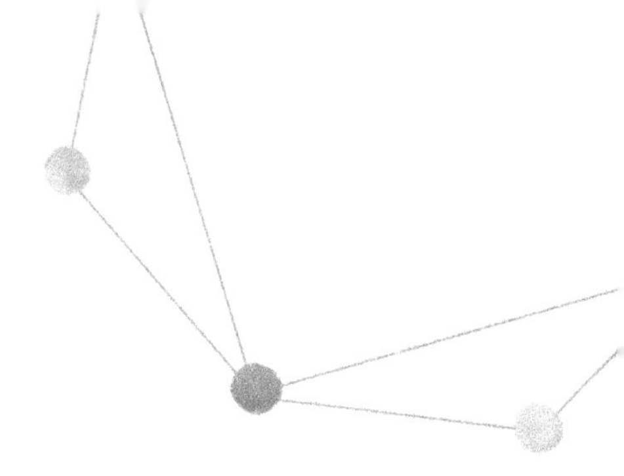

LOOKING TO WORK WITH JEN?

If you are a high-achieving female CXO or entrepreneur between the ages of 35 and 50 and you want to make a bigger impact or you're an organization interested in offering greater support to your teams and leaders—please contact me directly: Jen@jennash.com

DO YOU HAVE AN AMAZING STORY OF CONNECTION YOU WANT TO SHARE?

Did you meet someone randomly who changed your life? I'd love to hear about it.

Please share your stories (700 words or less) by emailing stories@jennash.com

References

1 Seppälä, Emma, Ph.D: *Social Connection Boosts Health, Even When You're Isolated.* March 2020, Psychology Today

2 Szalavitz, Maia: Touching Empathy. *Lack of physical attention can actually kill babies.* March 2010, Psychology Today

3 Loneliness Factsheet. https://www.cigna.com/static/www-cigna-com/docs/about-us/newsroom/studies-and-reports/combatting-loneliness/cigna-2020-loneliness-factsheet.pdf

4 Considerable.com (December 20, 2018). For some Japanese seniors, prison beats living alone/Fears of isolation and financial stress are driving some to commit petty crimes. https://www.considerable.com/life/caregiving/japanese-seniors-prison-beats-living-alone/

5 Health Resources & Services Administration, *The Loneliness Epidemic.* January 2019

6 Health Resources & Services Administration, *The Loneliness Epidemic.* January 2019

7 Rice University, News and Media Relations Office of Public Affairs: *How stress and loneliness can make you more likely to get COVID-19*

8 *Coronavirus Stress and Fear Could Take a Toll on Our Health.* PRB.org. May 14, 2020

9 Umberson D, Montez JK: *Social relationships and health: a flashpoint for health policy.* Journal of Health and Social Behavior. 2010;51

10 Umberson D, Montez JK: *Social relationships and health: a flashpoint for health policy.* Journal of Health and Social Behavior. 2010;51

11 Umberson D, Montez JK: *Social relationships and health: a flashpoint for health policy.* Journal of Health and Social Behavior. 2010;51

12 Uchino, Bert N: *Social support and health: a review of physiological processes potentially underlying links to disease outcomes.* Journal of Behavioral Medicine. August 2006; 29(4):377-87

13 Moynihan, Jan A., et al. *Psychosocial Factors and the Response to Influenza Vaccination in Older Adults.* Psychosomatic Medicine, vol. 66, no. 6, 2004, pp. 950-3.

14 Stanton, Brian: *How Human Connection Affects Our Health.* April 22, 2020. https://www.humnutrition.com/blog/human-connection-and-health/

15 Cacioppo JT, Cacioppo S: *Social Relationships and Health: The Toxic Effects of Perceived Social Isolation.* Social and personality psychology compass. February 2014 1;8(2):58-72.

16 Holt-Lunstad J, Smith TB, Layton JB: *Social relationships and mortality risk: a meta-analytic review.* PLOS Medicine. July 27, 2010

17 Stanton, Brian: *How Human Connection Affects Our Health.* April 22, 2020. https://www.humnutrition.com/blog/human-connection-and-health/

18 Applebury, Gabrielle: *Love and Life Advice for College Couples.* Love to Know. September 9, 2018. https://dating.lovetoknow.com/College_Couples

19 Carey, Kevin: *The Ivy League Students Least Likely To Get Married.* New York Times. March 29, 2019

20 Swedberg, Scott: *Is Landing a Job Really About Who You Know?* Dec 19, 2019. https://thejobsauce.com/is-landing-a-job-really-about-who-you-know/

21 Monster.co.uk: *Your professional networking questions – answered.* https://www.monster.co.uk/career-advice/article/what-is-networking-and-how-do-i-do-it

22 Umberson D, Montez JK: *Social relationships and health: a flashpoint for health policy.* Journal of Health and Social Behavior. 2010

23 Sarda-Joshi, Gauri: *Why chatting to strangers is good for you.* Brainfodder.org August 12 2016

24 Sandstrom, Gillian M., Why do people avoid talking to strangers? A mini meta-analysis of predicted fears and actual experiences talking to a stranger. Self & Identity Journal. Volume 20, 2021 - Issue 1: 25 Years of the Need to Belong. https://www.tandfonline.com/doi/full/10.1080/15298868.2020.1816568

25 Gauri, Sarda-Joshi, Gauri, (2016, August 12). Why chatting to strangers is good for you. Brainfodder.org. https://brainfodder.org/talking-to-strangers-benefits/

26 Sakulku, J: *The Impostor Phenomenon.* The Journal of Behavioral Science, 2011. 6(1), 75-97.

27 Tamir DI, Mitchell JP: *Disclosing information about the self is intrinsically rewarding.* Proceedings of the National Academy of Sciences of the United States of America. 2012;109(21).

28 Adler, Lou: *New Survey Reveals 85% of All Jobs are Filled Via Networking.* LinkedIn. Feburary 2, 2016

29 Patrick, Wendy L., J.D., Ph.D.: *How to Spark Powerful Chemistry Through Simple Conversation.* November 29, 2020

30 Contrary to popular belief Burning Man is not an art or music festival, instead it's a community that exists in Nevada, where it's built and collapsed for just a short period of time around the holiday known in The United States as Labor Day. Burning Man is a temporary city. People who take part understand that the organizers don't book acts or provide entertainment. What happens at Burning Man is up to attendees. They are entering a "DE commodified" space that values who they are, not what they have. Everyone is expected to collaborate, to be inclusive, creative, connective, and to clean up after themselves.

31 Bryant. Sean: *How Many Startups Fail and Why?* Investopedia.com. November 9, 2020.

32 Really helps to be wearing something a little loud so you make their job easy. A bright tie, a colorful jacket, unusual accessories. If you're all in black, gray, or navy—it's pretty hard to spot you across the room.

33 "Want Half My Orange?" was one of the book titles I strongly considered, because being generous is a great way to connect wholeheartedly with others around you.

34 See Kramar, E. J. J. and Lewis, Thomas B.: *Comparison of Visual and Nonvisual Listening.* Journal of Communication, November 1951, p. 16; and Heilman, Arthur W.: *An Investigation in Measuring and Improving Listening Ability of College Freshmen*, Speech Monographs, November 1951, p. 308.

35 Nichols, Ralph G. and Stevens, Leonard A.: *Listening to People*, Harvard Business Review, 1957

36 Cuncic, Arlin: *The Best Ways to Maintain Eye Contact.* Verywell Mind. 2019 https://www.verywellmind.com/how-do-i-maintain-good-eye-contact-3024392

37 Anderson, Cameron and Hildreth, John Angus D.: *Striving for superiority: The human desire for status.* IRLE Working Paper No. 115-16. 20156

38 Mann, Annamarie: *Why We Need Best Friends at Work*, GALLUP January 15, 2018 https://www.gallup.com/workplace/236213/why-need-best-friends-work.aspx

39 Horner, V., Whiten, A.: *Causal knowledge and imitation/emulation switching in chimpanzees (Pan troglodytes) and children (Homo sapiens). Anim Cogn* 8, 164–181. 2005.

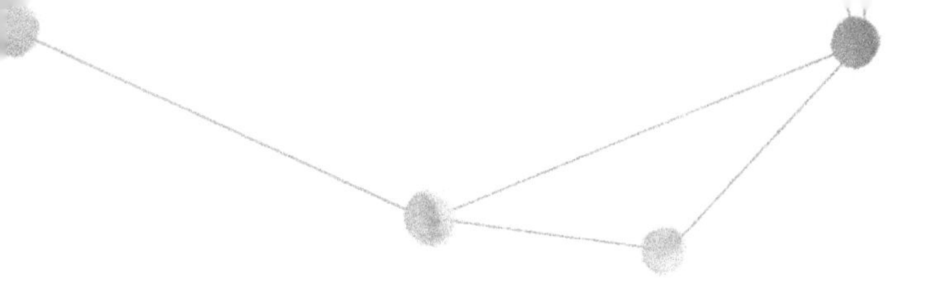

Jen Acknowledges

I'm thankful for a lot of things and a lot of people. I'm over the moon about honest conversations, crazy hot beverages, people who don't use technology as a shield, and the generous love and encouragement I got while writing this book from a few patient humans.

As my whole world crumbled alongside of everyone else's in 2019-2020, crushing my heart and many dreams—I gained so much clarity around how critical relational, whole-hearted connection is for every aspect of my being. The names Jen Collins, Jen Segalini, Daniel Nash, and Sylvia Deye must be shared as these top-notch humans kept reaching out, taking my calls, and telling me I could get this badboy written. Lisa Kalfus also deserves a long appreciative hug for holding so much space for me through the final publishing stages. Naturally, I owe a lot to Azul Terronez, his partner Steve Vannoy, and all the other members of my pod at *Authors Who Lead*. Together, they nurtured a colorful sketch into a book about powerful connections.

I'm also deeply grateful to my incredibly wise Wunderman posse (Tamara Upton, Lisa Burdige, Stacy Van Wickler, Kerry Mellor, Tracy Flynn Kubert and Ericka Robbins) for letting me go round and round on titles, subheads, and covers—when these powerhouse women didn't have any time to spare. And I tip my hat to Vernon Steward for sharing his amazing pointers on keeping relationships feeling fresh long-term. His ability to connect is second to none, and he has always inspired me.

It's wildly kind to offer to read someone's book and offer up notes, so I'm forever indebted to my early readers for their considered and nuanced feedback. Thank you to the lovely Lizzie Foster, Andrea Stringos, Dexter L. Jenks, Allison Graham, David Kidder, Toby O'Brien, Nina Chapin, Sterling Deye, Glenn Gentzke, Bill Carmody, and my awesome bonus kid Chelsea Yelk. You guys rock, and I owe you one.

I must thank my developmental editor Ann Maynard because she made a 'cute story' into a book that has the potential to impact people's lives. While I loved working with Ann because she made sticking to a schedule fun and achievable, I really loved how she insisted my tone and voice come to life page after page. It was so nice to feel seen, heard, and incredibly welcomed. A shout out to my copy editor Laura Kaiser whose copious and hilarious notes cheered me on through the slog of the editing, and to Jeanne Martinson at Wood Dragon Books who guided me through the publishing process. I'm also very appreciative for Rene Rossi's time. This fabulous PR maven, with a sharp wit and excellent connections, skillfully reached out to a Hollywood mega-producer who had excellent ideas on how to escape encounters gone wrong. Brandon Duncan, my talented recording and audio engineer, also deserves recognition for all his help getting my audio book done. From his patience with last-minute wordsmithing to his excellent home cooked meals, I feel blessed to know him and have him supporting me in this venture.

Last but not least I'm sending a HUGE shout out to all the humans that recognize themselves in the book. I'm glad your story was shared, and hopefully we'll inspire more connections, change more lives, and support awesome outcomes. People are the worst part of this world, but they are also the best part … so I remain ever hopeful and optimistic that more magical, awesome, and truly loving encounters await us all.

About the Author

As a Connector in Chief, Jen Nash helps people add more meaning to their lives through connections. She is a master facilitator, strategic advisor, author, sought-after executive coach and corporate speaker.

With over twenty years working as a senior consultant for Fortune 100 Pharma, Health, Tech, and Finance giants, Jen Nash now regularly inspires and supports Fortune 500 leaders to deepen their connections in support of all the good things in life: happiness, growth, and sustained community.

Born in Canada and raised around the world in such countries as Hong Kong, Tokyo, and Australia, Jennifer confuses people by speaking French with a French accent and trying her hands at over 40 other languages. She studied Communication Design at Parsons School of Design and The New School in New York City.

When not traveling the globe learning new ways to say 'thank you' and finding bright souls with whom to foster lifelong friendships, Jen Nash can be seen biking around New York City, Los Angeles, or striding around El Centro in San Miguel de Allende, Mexico.